LSAT Essentials:
The Ultimate Test Prep Guide

TST Scholastic Publishing

First published by TST Scholastic Publishing 2023

Copyright © 2023 by TST Scholastic Publishing

All rights reserved. No part of this publication may be reproduced, stored or transmitted in any form or by any means, electronic, mechanical, photocopying, recording, scanning, or otherwise without written permission from the publisher. It is illegal to copy this book, post it to a website, or distribute it by any other means without permission.

TST Scholastic Publishing asserts the moral right to be identified as the author of this work.

TST Scholastic Publishing has no responsibility for the persistence or accuracy of URLs for external or third-party Internet Websites referred to in this publication and does not guarantee that any content on such Websites is, or will remain, accurate or appropriate.

Designations used by companies to distinguish their products are often claimed as trademarks. All brand names and product names used in this book and on its cover are trade names, service marks, trademarks and registered trademarks of their respective owners. The publishers and the book are not associated with any product or vendor mentioned in this book. None of the companies referenced within the book have endorsed the book.

First edition

TABLE OF CONTENTS

I. INTRODUCTION
Chapter 1. LSAT Overview — 002
Chapter 2. LSAT Preparatory Guide Benefits — 004
Chapter 3. Guide Objectives and Structure — 006

II. LOGICAL REASONINING
Chapter 4. Understanding Logical Reasoning — 009
Chapter 5. Logical Reasoning Approach Strategies — 011
Chapter 6. Common Question Types and Techniques — 013
Chapter 7. Practice Exercise 1 — 015
Chapter 8. Practice Exercise 2 — 027
Chapter 9. Practice Exercise 1: Answers & Explanations — 040
Chapter 10. Practice Exercise 2: Answers & Explanations — 065

III. ANALYTICAL REASONING
Chapter 11. Introduction to the Analytical Reasoning — 091
Chapter 12. Techniques for Diagramming and Solving... — 092
Chapter 13. Strategies for Time Management and... — 094
Chapter 14. Practice Exercise 1 — 096
Chapeter 15. Practice Exercise 2 — 100
Chapter 16. Practice Exercise 1: Answers and Explanations — 104
Chapter 17. Practice Exercise 2: Answers and Explanations — 109

IV. READING COMPREHENSION
Chapter 18. Introduction to Reading Comprehension — 114
Chapter 19. Active Reading Strategies — 116
Chapter 20. Reading Comprehension Strategic Approaches — 118
Chapter 21. Reading Comprehension Exam Details — 120
Chapter 22. Practice Exam 1 — 122
Chapter 23. Practice Exam 2 — 131
Chapter 24. Practice Exam 1: Answers and Explanations — 140
Chapter 25. Practice Exam 2: Answers and Explanations — 168

V. WRITING SAMPLE
Chapter 26. Writing Sample Purpose and Evaluation Criteria — 197
Chapter 27. Structuring and Organizing a Persuasive Argument — 199
Chapter 28. Techniques for Developing Coherent Analysis... — 201
Chapter 29. Writing Sample Criteria — 203
Chapter 30. Practice Exercise 1 — 204
Chapter 31. Practice Exercise 2 — 205
Chapter 32. Practice Exercise #1 Sample Writing Answers — 206
Chapter 33. Practice Exercise #2 Sample Writing Answers — 209

TABLE OF CONTENTS

VI. LSAT TEST BEST PRACTICES
Chapter 34. Test Day Tips for Optimal Performance...   214
Chapter 35. Time Management Techniques...   217
Chapter 36. Guessing Strategies and the Impact on...   219
Chapter 37. Strategies for Reviewing and Analyzing...   221

VII. CONCLUSION
Chapter 38. Key Takeaways and Strategies...   224
Chapter 39. Final LSAT Success Advice   226
Chapter 40. Continued Practice and Self-Assessment...   228

I
Introduction

1

LSAT Overview

The Law School Admission Test (LSAT) is a standardized examination designed to assess the skills and abilities crucial for success in law school. Recognized and accepted by law schools in the United States, Canada, and other countries, the LSAT is fundamental to law school admissions. Its rigorous nature and comprehensive evaluation make it an essential consideration for admission committees when evaluating prospective law students.

The LSAT is highly regarded for its ability to measure the critical thinking, logical reasoning, analytical reasoning, and reading comprehension skills necessary for a legal education. By assessing these core abilities, the LSAT aims to provide law schools with a standardized and objective measure of an applicant's potential to excel in the demanding academic environment of law school.

Law schools emphasize LSAT scores as part of their holistic evaluation process. Alongside factors such as undergraduate GPA, letters of recommendation, and personal statements, LSAT scores allow admissions committees to gauge an applicant's readiness to tackle the intellectual challenges inherent in legal studies. A strong performance on the LSAT can enhance an applicant's chances of securing admission to their preferred law schools and even influence scholarship opportunities.

It is worth noting that while the LSAT is a crucial component of the law school admissions process, it is not the sole determinant of admission. Admissions committees take a holistic approach, considering multiple facets of an applicant's profile. However, a competitive LSAT score often significantly distinguishes applicants and highlights their aptitude for legal studies.

Given the weight placed on LSAT scores by law schools, adequate preparation and understanding of the test's format, question types, and strategies are crucial for aspiring law students. This LSAT preparatory guide, "LSAT Essentials: The Ultimate LSAT Prep Guide," aims to equip test takers with the knowledge, skills, and strategies necessary to excel on the LSAT and pursue their law school aspirations with confidence.

This guide will delve into each section of the LSAT—Logical Reasoning, Analytical Reasoning (Logic Games), Reading Comprehension, and the Writing Sample—providing comprehensive insights, strategies, and practice materials to help you navigate and master each component. Additionally, we will explore essential test-taking strategies, time management techniques, and resources for further support to ensure you are fully prepared for success on test day.

By diligently studying and applying the principles outlined in this guide, you can maximize your LSAT performance and strengthen your overall law school application. Remember, achieving your desired LSAT score requires dedication, practice, and a thorough understanding of the exam. With your commitment and the resources provided within this guide, you'll be able to start your journey toward law school with confidence and competence.

2

LSAT Preparatory Guide Benefits

A comprehensive LSAT preparation guide, such as "LSAT Essentials: The Ultimate LSAT Prep Guide," offers numerous advantages to individuals aspiring to excel on the LSAT and gain admission to reputable law schools. Understanding the benefits of utilizing a comprehensive LSAT preparation guide can help test takers make informed decisions about their study approach and maximize their chances of success. The following are some tangible benefits of utilizing such a guide:

- **Content Coverage:** A comprehensive LSAT preparation guide covers all sections of the LSAT, including Logical Reasoning, Analytical Reasoning (Logic Games), Reading Comprehension, and the Writing Sample. It provides in-depth explanations, strategies, and practice materials specific to each section, ensuring comprehensive content coverage.

- **Test Familiarization:** The LSAT preparation guide acquaints test takers with the format, structure, and question types encountered in the exam. By providing sample questions and practice exercises, the guide enables individuals to become familiar with the specific challenges presented by each section, enhancing their confidence and reducing test anxiety.

- **Strategy Development:** The guide equips test takers with practical strategies and techniques to approach different question types and maximize their performance. It provides step-by-step instructions, tips, and shortcuts for logical reasoning, diagramming logic games, tackling reading comprehension passages, and crafting persuasive arguments for the writing sample.

- **Skill Enhancement:** A comprehensive LSAT preparation guide facilitates developing and refining critical skills essential for success on the LSAT. It emphasizes improving critical thinking, analytical reasoning, logical reasoning, and reading comprehension abilities through targeted exercises and practice drills.

- **Time Management:** The LSAT preparation guide offers valuable insights and strategies for managing time efficiently during the exam. It provides techniques for pacing oneself, making educated guesses, and allocating time appropriately across different sections, helping test takers optimize their performance within the given time constraints.

- **Performance Evaluation:** The guide includes practice tests and exercises with detailed answer explanations, allowing test takers to assess their strengths and weaknesses. By providing feedback on performance and highlighting areas requiring further attention, the guide aids in identifying and addressing specific skill gaps, enhancing overall test readiness.

- **Confidence Building:** Utilizing a comprehensive LSAT preparation guide instills confidence in test takers by providing them with a structured study plan, clear guidance, and ample practice opportunities. Increased confidence contributes to reduced test anxiety, improved focus, and a positive mindset, ultimately enhancing performance on test day.

- **Supplemental Resources:** The LSAT preparation guide may recommend additional esources, such as official LSAC materials, online courses, tutoring services, or study groups. These resources can further support test takers' LSAT preparation, offering alternative perspectives, additional practice materials, and expert guidance.

By leveraging the benefits offered by a comprehensive LSAT preparation guide, test takers can optimize their study efforts, develop essential skills, and enhance their overall performance on the LSAT. It is important to note that each individual's experience may vary, and active engagement with the provided strategies and resources is critical to achieving desired outcomes.

3

Guide Objectives and Structure

"LSAT Essentials: The Ultimate LSAT Prep Guide" is designed to assist test takers in comprehensively preparing for each section of the LSAT: Logical Reasoning, Analytical Reasoning (Logic Games), Reading Comprehension, and the Writing Sample. The guide is structured to align with the specific format and content of the LSAT, providing a systematic approach to mastering the exam.

The objectives of the guide are to provide a comprehensive understanding of the LSAT's importance in law school admissions, equip test takers with practical strategies and techniques for approaching different question types, develop and enhance critical thinking, analytical reasoning, logical reasoning, and reading comprehension skills, improve time management abilities to maximize performance within the given time constraints, guide test takers in crafting well-structured and persuasive arguments for the Writing Sample, and foster confidence and reduce test anxiety through familiarity with the LSAT format and question types.

The guide is organized as follows:

- **Introduction:** The introduction provides an overview of the LSAT's significance in law school admissions and explains the guide's objectives and structure.

- **Logical Reasoning:** This section introduces the Logical Reasoning section and offers explanations of question types, along with strategies for approaching them. It includes practice exercises with detailed explanations.

- **Analytical Reasoning (Logic Games):** The section on Analytical Reasoning (Logic Games) provides an introduction to this section of the LSAT, techniques for diagramming and solving different types of logic games, strategies for time management and efficiency, and sample games with step-by-step explanations and practice drills.

- **Reading Comprehension:** In this section, an overview of the Reading Comprehension section is given, along with active reading strategies for comprehending complex passages, approaches for identifying main ideas, structures, and author's perspective, and practice exercises with detailed answer explanations.

- **Writing Sample:** The Writing Sample section explains the requirements of this section and provides techniques for analyzing and arguing for one of two options. It also includes sample prompts and model responses for practice.

- **LSAT Test Strategies:** This section offers test day tips for optimal performance and stress management, time management techniques for each section, guessing strategies and their impact on scoring, and strategies for reviewing and analyzing practice tests.

- **Additional Resources and Support:** The guide recommends study materials, including official LSAC resources, and provides an overview of online courses, tutoring services, and study groups. It also offers strategies for maintaining motivation and managing study schedules, along with guidance on seeking further assistance and support.

- **Conclusion:** The conclusion section recaps key takeaways and strategies covered in the guide, provides final words of encouragement and advice for LSAT success, and emphasizes the importance of continued practice and self-assessment.

By following the structure of the guide, test takers can systematically address each section of the LSAT, acquire essential skills and strategies, and build confidence in their ability to excel on the exam.

II
Logical Reasoning

4

Understanding Logical Reasoning

Logical Reasoning is a critical component of the LSAT that assesses an individual's ability to analyze and evaluate arguments. This section presents a series of short passages followed by a question or set of questions. To effectively approach Logical Reasoning questions, it is essential to understand their purpose and underlying structure.

Purpose: Logical Reasoning questions are designed to evaluate a test taker's ability to analyze, critically assess, and draw logical conclusions from arguments. These questions assess skills such as recognizing argument structures, identifying flaws in reasoning, evaluating evidence, and applying logical principles to reach sound conclusions. The primary objective is to measure the ability to think critically and make reasoned judgments, which are fundamental skills for success in legal studies.

Structure: Logical Reasoning questions typically consist of a stimulus—an argument presented as a short passage—and one or more accompanying questions. The stimulus may present an argument, a set of facts, or both. Each question requires test takers to analyze the stimulus and select the most appropriate response from the given answer choices.

- **Stimulus Analysis:** Understanding the stimulus is crucial for answering Logical Reasoning questions accurately. Test takers should carefully read and analyze the passage, paying attention to the main point, the author's position, and the supporting evidence or reasoning provided. Identifying the underlying structure of the argument, including premises and conclusions, helps recognize its strengths or weaknesses.

- **Question Types:** Logical Reasoning questions encompass various types, including strengthen, weaken, assumption, inference, and flaw questions, among others. Each question type tests a different aspect of critical reasoning and requires a specific approach. Familiarity with the different question types and their respective characteristics is essential for effectively tackling them.

- **Answer Choice Evaluation:** Test takers evaluate the answer choices after comprehending the stimulus and question stem. The options may include attractive distractors that appear plausible but ultimately weaken the argument or fail to address the question properly. Understanding the subtle nuances and potential pitfalls within answer choices is crucial for proper selection.

- **Reasoning Patterns**: Logical Reasoning questions often exhibit recurring reasoning patterns, such as conditional statements, cause-and-effect relationships, analogies, and counterarguments. Recognizing and understanding these patterns can help test takers quickly identify the underlying logic and effectively navigate the question.

- **Time Management:** Time management is crucial in the Logical Reasoning section. Since each question carries equal weight, maintaining a steady pace is essential to complete the section within the allotted time. Developing efficient strategies, such as identifying more straightforward questions to tackle first or flagging challenging questions for later review, can aid in optimizing time utilization.

Test takers can approach this section of the LSAT with clarity and confidence by comprehending the purpose and structure of Logical Reasoning questions. Understanding the stimulus, recognizing question types, evaluating answer choices, and managing time effectively are critical strategies for success. With consistent practice and familiarity with various reasoning patterns, test takers can refine their analytical skills and enhance their performance on the Logical Reasoning section of the LSAT.

5

Logical Reasoning Approach Strategies

In the Logical Reasoning section of the LSAT, test takers are presented with a variety of arguments that require careful analysis and evaluation. Developing effective strategies for approaching and analyzing arguments is essential for success in this section. The following strategies can aid test takers in comprehensively tackling Logical Reasoning questions:

- **Read Actively:** When encountering a stimulus, read actively and attentively. Pay close attention to the main point of the argument, the author's position, and the supporting evidence or reasoning provided. Underline or take brief notes to highlight key elements and identify the argument's structure.

- **Identify the Argument Structure**: Recognizing the structure of the argument is crucial. Identify the premises (statements that provide support or evidence) and the conclusion (the main claim or the point the author is making). Understanding the relationship between the premises and the conclusion helps evaluate the argument's logical strength.

- **Question Stem Analysis:** Carefully analyze the question stem to determine the specific task being asked. Different question types require different approaches, such as identifying assumptions, finding flaws, drawing inferences, or evaluating the argument's strength. Understanding the question stem helps focus on the argument's relevant aspects.

- **Prephrase and Predict:** Before evaluating the answer choices, prephrase or predict the response that you expect to be correct. This prethinking process helps in focusing your attention and forming expectations based on the information provided in the stimulus. It can guide you in selecting the most appropriate answer choice.

- **Evaluate Answer Choices Systematically:** Thoroughly evaluate each answer choice, considering its relevance to the question stem and the information provided in the stimulus. Eliminate choices that are out of scope, contradict the argument, or do not sufficiently address the question being asked. Compare the remaining choices to identify the most accurate and logical response.

- **Be Mindful of Logical Fallacies and Flaws:** Logical Reasoning questions often present arguments with underlying flaws or fallacies. Develop familiarity with common logical fallacies, such as circular reasoning, false causation, or ad hominem attacks. Identifying and pointing out these flaws can lead to the correct answer choice.

- **Manage Time Effectively:** The Logical Reasoning section requires efficient time management. Allocate appropriate time for each question and avoid getting stuck on difficult or time-consuming ones. If uncertain, make an educated guess and move on to ensure that you address all questions within the time constraints.

- **Practice and Review:** Regular practice and review are crucial for honing your skills in analyzing arguments. Work through various practice questions and review the explanations for correct and incorrect answers. Pay attention to patterns, strategies, and reasoning approaches used in different question types to enhance your analytical abilities.

Test takers can effectively approach and analyze arguments in the LSAT's Logical Reasoning section using these strategies. Active reading, identifying argument structure, analyzing question stems, prethinking, systematic evaluation of answer choices, recognizing logical fallacies, managing time, and consistent practice all contribute to developing strong analytical skills necessary for success on the LSAT.

6

Common Question Types and Techniques

In the Logical Reasoning section of the LSAT, test takers encounter a variety of question types that require distinct approaches and techniques. Familiarizing oneself with these question types and employing effective strategies for each can significantly enhance performance. The following outlines common question types and their corresponding techniques:

Strengthen/Weaken Questions: Strengthen and weaken questions require test takers to identify answer choices that either strengthen or weaken the argument presented in the stimulus. Effective techniques include:

- Assessing the Gap: Identify the gap or logical leap between the premises and the conclusion. Look for answer choices that fill in the gap or undermine the reasoning, respectively.

- Analyzing Cause and Effect: Determine whether the evidence adequately supports the causal relationship presented in the argument. Evaluate answer choices that provide additional evidence or challenge the causal link.

Assumption Questions: Assumption questions focus on identifying unstated assumptions necessary for the argument's validity. Key techniques include:

- Bridging the Gap: Identify the underlying assumptions that connect the premises to the conclusion. Look for answer choices that make the argument logically coherent by filling in the missing information.

- Negation Test: Negate each answer choice and assess its impact on the argument. If negating an answer choice weakens the argument, it is likely an underlying assumption.

Inference Questions: Inference questions require test takers to draw logical conclusions based on the information presented in the stimulus. Strategies for these questions include:

- Staying Within the Bounds: Focus on answer choices that can be reasonably drawn from the information provided. Avoid extreme or exaggerated options.

- Identifying Supported Statements: Look for answer choices that are directly supported by the evidence or that necessarily follow from the argument's structure.

Flaw Questions: Flaw questions assess the argument's weaknesses, errors, or logical fallacies. Effective techniques for these questions include:

- Recognizing Common Fallacies: Familiarize yourself with common logical fallacies, such as circular reasoning, false analogy, or ad hominem attacks. Identify answer choices that highlight these flaws.

- Comparing Standards of Reasoning: Evaluate the argument against recognized standards of good reasoning. Look for answer choices that point out deviations from logical principles.

Parallel Reasoning Questions: Parallel reasoning questions require test takers to identify answer choices that exhibit similar reasoning structures to the one presented in the stimulus. Strategies for these questions include:

- Identifying the Logical Structure: Analyze the logical structure of the stimulus, focusing on the relationship between the premises and the conclusion. Select answer choices with similar structures.

- Negation Test: Negate the premises and conclusion in the stimulus and the answer choices to evaluate whether the logical relationship is preserved.

Principle Questions: Principle questions assess the ability to apply general principles to a given situation. Techniques for these questions include:

- Analyzing the Principle: Identify the underlying principle presented in the stimulus. Look for answer choices that adhere to the same principle when applied to a new scenario.

- Evaluating Analogies: Assess how well the principle in the stimulus applies to a parallel situation described in the answer choices.

Understanding the characteristics of these common question types and employing appropriate techniques can significantly enhance performance in the Logical Reasoning section of the LSAT. By practicing with a variety of question types and refining these strategies, test takers can navigate the complexity of each question type more effectively, leading to more accurate and confident responses.

7
Practice Exercise 1

Stimulus #1:

A recent study found that individuals who regularly engage in physical exercise have a lower risk of developing heart disease. Therefore, it is clear that incorporating regular exercise into one's lifestyle is crucial for maintaining a healthy heart.

Question Stem:

Which of the following, if true, would most seriously weaken the argument?

Answer Choices:

A.) Most heart disease cases are primarily caused by genetic factors.
B.) The study did not differentiate between different types of physical exercise.
C.) Individuals who engage in physical exercise have a higher likelihood of developing other health problems.
D.) The study only considered individuals between the ages of 20 and 30.
E.) The study did not account for dietary habits and other lifestyle factors.

*　*　*

Stimulus #2:

All philosophers are thinkers. Socrates is a philosopher.

Question Stem:

Which of the following conclusions is most strongly supported by the statements above?

Answer Choices:

A.) Socrates is a thinker.
B.) All thinkers are philosophers.
C.) Socrates is not a thinker.
D.) Socrates could be a musician.

E.) All philosophers are Socrates.

* * *

Stimulus #3:

Every member of the soccer team attended the meeting. If Lisa attended the meeting, then Lisa is a member of the soccer team.

Question Stem:

Which of the following conclusions is most strongly supported by the statements above?

Answer Choices:

A.) If Lisa is not a member of the soccer team, then Lisa did not attend the meeting.
B.) Every member of the soccer team is named Lisa.
C.) Lisa is the only member of the soccer team.
D.) If Lisa did not attend the meeting, she is not a member of the soccer team.
E.) If you are not Lisa, then you are not a member of the soccer team.

* * *

Stimulus #4:

If the rain continues, the game will be postponed. The game was not postponed.

Question Stem:

Which of the following conclusions is most strongly supported by the statements above?

Answer Choices:

A.) It did not continue to rain.
B.) The game was held in the rain.
C.) The rain stopped before the game.
D.) The game was canceled.
E.) It was sunny during the game.

* * *

Stimulus #5:

All novelists are creative. Some novelists are not patient.

Question Stem:

Which of the following conclusions is most strongly supported by the statements above?

Answer Choices:

A.) Some creative people are not patient.
B.) All patient people are novelists.
C.) All creative people are novelists.
D.) Some patient people are not creative.
E.) No patient person is creative.

* * *

Stimulus #6:

Every employee at the firm works either in Accounting or in Marketing. No one in Marketing works on weekends. Sarah works on weekends.

Question Stem:

Which of the following conclusions is most strongly supported by the statements above?

Answer Choices:

A.) Sarah works in Marketing.
B.) Sarah works in Accounting.
C.) Sarah does not work at the firm.
D.) Everyone who works on weekends is in Accounting.
E.) No one in Accounting works on weekends.

* * *

Stimulus #7:

All cats are animals. No plants are animals. Some trees are plants.

Question Stem:

Which of the following conclusions is most strongly supported by the statements above?

Answer Choices:

A.) Some trees are cats.
B.) No cats are trees.
C.) Some plants are cats.
D.) All animals are trees.
E.) No trees are animals.

***

Stimulus #8:

The company policy states that if an employee works more than 40 hours in a week, that employee will receive overtime pay. Last week, Jackson did not receive overtime pay.

Question Stem:

Which of the following conclusions is most strongly supported by the statements above?

Answer Choices:

A.) Jackson is not an employee of the company.
B.) Jackson worked 40 hours or less last week.
C.) Jackson worked more than 40 hours last week.
D.) Jackson received less pay than he should have.
E.) The company policy does not apply to Jackson.

***

Stimulus #9:

All roses are flowers. Some flowers are red. Therefore, some roses are red.

Question Stem:

Which of the following, if true, would most strengthen the argument?

Answer Choices:

A.) Some roses are not red.
B.) All roses are red.
C.) All red things are flowers.
D.) Some flowers are not red.
E.) Some red things are roses.

***

Stimulus #10:

Every citizen of Town X lives in either the Northside or the Southside district. Last year, the crime rate in the Northside district was twice as high as that in the Southside district. John, a citizen of Town X, was a victim of a crime last year.

Question Stem:

Which of the following conclusions is most strongly supported by the statements above?

Answer Choices:

A.) John lives in the Northside district.
B.) Crime rates in Town X are higher than average.
C.) John is more likely to be a victim of a crime this year.
D.) John was a victim of two crimes last year.
E.) John may live in the Southside district.

***

Stimulus #11:

All dogs bark. Some animals that bark are not aggressive. Therefore, some dogs are not aggressive.

Question Stem:

Which of the following, if true, would most strengthen the argument?

Answer Choices:

A.) Some aggressive animals do not bark.
B.) All dogs are animals.
C.) All animals that bark are dogs.
D.) Some dogs are aggressive.
E.) Some non-aggressive animals are dogs.

***

Stimulus #12:

In City A, the average rainfall per year is higher than that in City B. However, last year, City B had more rainy days than City A.

Question Stem:

Which of the following conclusions is most strongly supported by the statements above?

Answer Choices:

A.) Rainfall in City B is more evenly distributed throughout the year.
B.) Rainfall in City A is more intense when it does rain.
C.) City B had a wetter year than City A last year.
D.) The climate in City B is wetter than in City A.
E.) City A will have more rainy days than City B this year.

* * *

Stimulus #13:

All athletes must maintain a healthy diet. Anyone who does not eat enough protein is not maintaining a healthy diet. Sam, an athlete, eats plenty of protein.

Question Stem:

Which of the following, if true, would most weaken the argument?

Answer Choices:

A.) Sam does not consume enough carbohydrates.
B.) Sam has won several sports competitions.
C.) Sam takes protein supplements daily.
D.) Sam is considered one of the best athletes in his school.
E.) Sam also includes fruits and vegetables in his diet.

* * *

Stimulus #14:

Most successful business people read the daily financial news. Jane wants to become a successful businessperson. Jane has just subscribed to several daily financial news sources.

Question Stem:

Which of the following conclusions is most strongly supported by the statements above?

Answer Choices:

A.) Reading the daily financial news will make Jane a successful businessperson.
B.) Jane will become a successful businessperson.
C.) Jane is a successful businessperson.
D.) Jane is more likely to become a successful businessperson than before she subscribed to the financial news.
E.) Jane subscribed to the financial news because most successful business people do.

***

Stimulus #15:

No vegetables are fruits. All apples are fruits. Thus, no apples are vegetables.

Question Stem:

Which of the following, if true, would most strengthen the argument?

Answer Choices:

A.) Some vegetables are green.
B.) All fruits are not vegetables.
C.) Some apples are red.
D.) No fruits are green.
E.) All green things are vegetables.

***

Stimulus #16:

Most writers who have won the Pulitzer Prize for Fiction have studied literature at a university level. Charles, who studied literature at a prestigious university and has written multiple critically acclaimed short stories, has just completed his first novel.

Question Stem:

Which of the following conclusions is most strongly supported by the statements above?

Answer Choices:

A.) Charles will win the Pulitzer Prize for Fiction.
B.) Charles' novel will be a bestseller.
C.) Charles is likely to become a professor of literature at a university.
D.) Charles has a greater chance of winning the Pulitzer Prize for Fiction than a writer who has not studied literature at a university or written critically acclaimed stories.
E.) Charles will write another novel.

***

Stimulus #17:

People who consume fast food more than three times a week have a higher risk of developing obesity. John, a professional athlete, eats fast food four times a week.

Question Stem:

Which of the following, if true, would most weaken the argument?

Answer Choices:

A.) John's athletic profession requires him to train rigorously every day.
B.) John prefers fast food to home-cooked meals.
C.) People who exercise regularly can still develop obesity.
D.) The study did not consider the lifestyle or physical activity levels of the subjects.
E.) Fast food is a major contributor to the global obesity epidemic.

***

Stimulus #18:

Several studies indicate that young children who are exposed to multiple languages in their early years tend to have more advanced cognitive skills than their monolingual counterparts. Additionally, it's found that these children perform better in problem-solving tasks. Claire, a 4-year-old, is growing up in a bilingual household where her parents regularly speak both English and Spanish.

Question Stem:

Which of the following conclusions is most strongly supported by the statements above?

Answer Choices:

A.) Claire will outperform all her peers in cognitive tasks.
B.) Claire will become a translator when she grows up.
C.) All bilingual children are smarter than monolingual children.
D.) Claire is likely to have more advanced cognitive skills and better problem-solving abilities compared to some monolingual children her age.
E.) Claire's parents are language teachers.

***

Stimulus #19:

Cities with higher rates of public transportation use tend to have lower rates of obesity. Boston, a city known for its extensive public transportation system, has seen a recent surge in obesity rates.

Question Stem:

Which of the following, if true, would most help to explain the apparent paradox?

Answer Choices:

A.) Boston's public transportation system has been facing frequent service disruptions recently.
B.) Most cities with low rates of obesity have a well-established healthcare system.
C.) Boston has the largest public transportation system in the country.
D.) Obesity rates are generally higher in cities with colder climates.
E.) A significant portion of Boston's population prefers driving over using public transportation.

***

Stimulus #20:

Company Z is an online retailer that recently implemented a customer loyalty program offering discounts to repeat customers. The expectation was to see an increase in sales as a result. However, after the introduction of the program, the company experienced a decrease in overall sales.

Question Stem:

Which of the following, if true, would most help to explain the apparent paradox?

Answer Choices:

A.) Many customers of Company Z made bulk purchases before the implementation of the loyalty program.
B.) Company Z's competitors do not offer any customer loyalty programs.
C.) Company Z's customer loyalty program is very complex and difficult to understand.
D.) The products offered by Company Z are of high quality.
E.) Some customers of Company Z do not make purchases frequently.

***

Stimulus #21:

The best way to foster a love of art in children is to expose them to artworks at a young age. Thus, school curricula should include regular visits to art museums.

Question Stem:

The argument depends on which of the following assumptions?

Answer Choices:

A.) All children will develop a love for art if exposed to artworks at a young age.
B.) Art museums are the only places where children can be exposed to artworks.
C.) Regular visits to art museums will guarantee a love for art in all children.
D.) Exposure to art at a young age can influence a child's appreciation of art.
E.) School curricula currently lack sufficient exposure to art.

***

Stimulus #22:

Most residents of City X, who live near the old factory, complain about air pollution. Hence, the old factory is likely the source of the air pollution in City X.

Question Stem:

Which of the following is most similar in its reasoning to the argument above?

Answer Choices:

A.) Many people who enjoy playing sports also follow sports news, so playing sports causes interest in sports news.
B.) The majority of students in School Y, who eat in the cafeteria, complain about stomachaches. Therefore, the cafeteria food is probably causing the stomachaches.
C.) As many people who live in City Z complain about traffic, there must be a lot of cars in City Z.
D.) Many residents of City W, who work in the downtown area, complain about noise pollution. Therefore, the downtown area is too noisy.
E.) Most visitors to Park K, who picnic near the lake, complain about mosquitoes. Hence, the lake is infested with mosquitoes.

* * *

Stimulus #23:

John argues: "Since all fruits are good sources of vitamins and apples are fruits, apples are good sources of vitamins."

Question Stem:

Which one of the following principles, if valid, would most help to justify John's reasoning?

Answer Choices:

A.) Everything that belongs to a certain category shares all the features of that category.
B.) Apples are the best source of vitamins among all fruits.
C.) If something is a good source of vitamins, it must be a fruit.
D.) Only fruits are good sources of vitamins.
E.) Fruits that are not good sources of vitamins are not truly fruits.

* * *

Stimulus #24:

The local theater company is planning to stage a play next month. However, the last three plays staged by the company did not attract a large audience. Therefore, it is unlikely that the play next month will draw a significant crowd.

Question Stem:

Which of the following, if true, would most strengthen the argument?

Answer Choices:

A.) The local theater company has been around for more than 20 years.
B.) The play being staged next month is written by a very popular and acclaimed playwright.
C.) Many regular theater-goers have expressed disappointment with the recent performances of the local theater company.
D.) The theater where the play will be staged has been recently renovated.
E.) The theater company has a new director with an innovative approach to staging plays.

※ ※ ※

Stimulus #25:

Despite having a higher number of registered vehicles, Country X has fewer annual traffic accidents than Country Y.

Question Stem:

Which of the following, if true, would best explain the paradox?

Answer Choices:

A.) Country X has more urban areas than Country Y.
B.) The population of Country Y is significantly smaller than that of Country X.
C.) The drivers in Country X are required to undergo a rigorous driving test before obtaining their licenses.
D.) Country X has a significantly larger land area than Country Y.
E.) Country Y has a higher percentage of elderly drivers than Country X.

8
Practice Exercise 2

Stimulus #1:

Whenever I eat at Restaurant A, I have an upset stomach. I ate at Restaurant A last night and now I have an upset stomach. Therefore, the food from Restaurant A is the cause of my upset stomach.

Question Stem:

Which one of the following arguments is most similar in its reasoning to the argument above?

Answer Choices:

A.) I always get a headache when I study for too long. I studied for five hours yesterday and now I have a headache. Therefore, studying for long hours is the cause of my headache.
B.) Every time it rains, my car won't start. It rained yesterday and my car won't start today. Therefore, the rain causes my car's engine to malfunction.
C.) I always get a fever when I catch a cold. I have a fever today, so I must have a cold.
D.) Whenever I drink coffee, I feel more alert. I drank coffee this morning and I feel alert. Therefore, coffee is a stimulant.
E.) Every time I eat spicy food, I get heartburn. I ate spicy food yesterday and today I don't have heartburn. Therefore, spicy food isn't the cause of my heartburn.

∗ ∗ ∗

Stimulus #2:

Many who use public transportation complain about the service. However, the number of passengers using public transportation has been steadily increasing over the last few years. Therefore, the complaints about public transportation are unwarranted.

Question Stem:

Which of the following most accurately describes the flaw in the argument?

Answer Choices:

A.) It fails to consider that the increase in passengers might be due to factors other than the quality of the service.
B.) It assumes that all passengers have the same standards for public transportation.
C.) It fails to provide evidence that complaints have decreased as the number of passengers increased.
D.) It assumes that an increase in the number of passengers means an increase in satisfaction.
E.) It fails to consider that more passengers might lead to more complaints.

* * *

Stimulus #3:

All university students must complete a mathematics course to graduate. John is a university student. Therefore, if John does not complete a mathematics course, he will not graduate.

Question Stem:

The argument above assumes which one of the following?

Answer Choices:

A.) John wants to graduate.
B.) John has not yet completed a mathematics course.
C.) Every university student must take the same mathematics course.
D.) There are no exceptions to the graduation requirement of completing a mathematics course.
E.) John is incapable of completing a mathematics course.

* * *

Stimulus #4:

Only employees who have worked at the company for more than 5 years are eligible for the loyalty bonus. Susan has worked at the company for 7 years.

Question Stem:

Which one of the following can be properly inferred from the statements above?

Answer Choices:

A.) Susan has received the loyalty bonus.
B.) Susan is not eligible for the loyalty bonus.
C.) Susan is eligible for the loyalty bonus.

D.) All employees who have worked for the company for more than 5 years receive the loyalty bonus.
E.) Susan has been with the company longer than any other employee.

* * *

Stimulus #5:

No fruits are low in vitamins because all fruits are nutritious, and anything that is nutritious is not low in vitamins.

Question Stem:

Which one of the following arguments is most similar in its reasoning to the argument above?

Answer Choices:

A.) All mammals are warm-blooded, and all cats are mammals. Therefore, all cats are warm-blooded.
B.) No cars are cheap because all cars are machines, and all machines are expensive.
C.) All dogs are animals, and all animals need food. Therefore, all dogs need food.
D.) No chairs are comfortable because all chairs are furniture, and all furniture is uncomfortable.
E.) All fish live in water, and all sharks are fish. Therefore, all sharks live in water.

* * *

Stimulus #6:

The new law has not had any significant effect on crime rates. Therefore, the law was not necessary.

Question Stem:

Which one of the following identifies a flaw in the reasoning above?

Answer Choices:

A.) The argument presumes, without providing justification, that the only purpose of the law was to affect crime rates.
B.) The argument fails to consider that crime rates may have risen if the law had not been enacted.
C.) The argument assumes that the new law should have had an immediate impact on crime rates.
D.) The argument overlooks the possibility that the law may have other benefits that are not related to crime rates.
E.) All of the above.

* * *

Stimulus #7:

John: The internet provides a convenient way for people to shop without leaving their homes, and therefore, e-commerce is undoubtedly the future of shopping. Sara: But many people still prefer the tangible experience of physical shopping, not to mention the immediate gratification of getting their purchases right away.

Question Stem:

John and Sara disagree over whether:

Answer Choices:

A.) The internet is convenient for shopping.
B.) Physical shopping provides immediate gratification.
C.) E-commerce is the future of shopping.
D.) People prefer the tangible experience of physical shopping.
E.) E-commerce and physical shopping can coexist.

***

Stimulus #8:

If Mary studies for the exam, she will pass. Mary didn't pass the exam.

Question Stem:

If the above statements are true, which one of the following must also be true?

Answer Choices:

A.) Mary didn't study for the exam.
B.) Mary studied for the exam.
C.) The exam was too difficult.
D.) Mary never studies for exams.
E.) Mary is not good at exams.

***

Stimulus #9:

Jack believes that anyone who wants to be successful in life needs to first learn how to deal with failure.

Question Stem:

Which one of the following principles, if valid, most helps to justify Jack's belief?

Answer Choices:

A.) The path to success is paved with countless failures.
B.) One's ability to handle success is indicative of their character.
C.) Failure should be avoided at all costs to be successful.
D.) Success comes to those who work the hardest.
E.) Success and failure are unrelated.

***

Stimulus #10:

All of the fruit from a certain tree were counted. There were more apples than oranges, but when half of the apples and half of the oranges fell from the tree, there were more oranges than apples remaining on the tree.

Question Stem:

Which one of the following, if true, most helps to explain the paradoxical situation described above?

Answer Choices:

A.) The oranges were smaller than the apples.
B.) More than half of the apples fell from the tree.
C.) The oranges were more tightly attached to the tree than the apples.
D.) The apples and oranges were counted incorrectly the first time.
E.) The tree produces more oranges in a year than apples.

***

Stimulus #11:

All the great artists of the Renaissance were patrons of the Medici family. Leonardo da Vinci did not receive patronage from the Medici family.

Question Stem:

If all the statements above are true, which one of the following must also be true?

Answer Choices:

A.) Leonardo da Vinci was not a great artist of the Renaissance.
B.) The Medici family were the only patrons of great artists in the Renaissance.
C.) Leonardo da Vinci received patronage from another family.
D.) The Medici family did not appreciate Leonardo da Vinci's art.
E.) Leonardo da Vinci was a great artist of the Renaissance.

***

Stimulus #12:

If a movie receives critical acclaim, then it has excellent cinematography. However, just because a movie has excellent cinematography does not mean it will receive critical acclaim.

Question Stem:

Which one of the following arguments is most similar in its reasoning to the argument above?

Answer Choices:

A.) If a book is a bestseller, then it is well-written. But a well-written book will not necessarily be a bestseller.
B.) If a painting is famous, it must be old. However, not all old paintings are famous.
C.) If a song is catchy, it will be popular. But not all popular songs are catchy.
D.) If a play is long, it must be boring. But not all long plays are boring.
E.) If a car is expensive, it must be luxurious. But not all luxurious cars are expensive.

***

Stimulus #13:

All government policies should be guided by the principle of the greatest good for the greatest number of people. However, a recent policy has resulted in significant benefits for a small minority, but negative effects for the majority.

Question Stem:

Which of the following principles, if valid, would most undermine the reasoning of the policy?

Answer Choices:

A.) The needs of the many outweigh the needs of the few.
B.) Minority rights should be protected at all costs.
C.) Any policy that benefits some at the expense of others is unjust.
D.) The majority is not always right.
E.) Policy should first do no harm.

***

Stimulus #14:

A recent study found that people who exercise regularly are more likely to catch a cold than those who do not exercise at all. However, regular exercise is known to boost the immune system.

Question Stem:

Which one of the following, if true, most helps to resolve the apparent paradox?

Answer Choices:

A.) The study did not take into account the dietary habits of the subjects.
B.) People who exercise regularly are more likely to engage in outdoor activities, where they are more exposed to cold viruses.
C.) Regular exercise reduces stress levels.
D.) The study included only a small sample of people.
E.) Not all people who exercise regularly maintain a balanced diet.

***

Stimulus #15:

In order to encourage healthier eating habits, a school has decided to ban all high-sugar snacks from its premises. The principal argues that this move will decrease the overall sugar intake of the students.

Question Stem:

The principal's argument relies on which of the following assumptions?

Answer Choices:

A.) The students will not bring high-sugar snacks from home.
B.) The students do not prefer high-sugar snacks.
C.) The school was the primary source of high-sugar snacks for the students.
D.) The students do not consume high-sugar snacks outside of school.
E.) The school can effectively enforce the ban on high-sugar snacks.

* * *

Stimulus #16:

A survey shows that people who listen to classical music are more likely to score higher on IQ tests than those who listen to other genres. Therefore, listening to classical music increases one's IQ.

Question Stem:

Which one of the following, if true, would most weaken the argument?

Answer Choices:

A.) IQ tests are not the only measure of intelligence.
B.) People who listen to classical music also tend to engage in other activities known to increase intelligence, such as reading.
C.) Classical music is often played in environments that stimulate intellectual activity.
D.) People who score higher on IQ tests also tend to earn more money.
E.) The majority of high IQ individuals reported that they prefer classical music over other genres.

* * *

Stimulus #17:

Cafe Mocha argued that their coffee is superior because they use Arabica beans, which are more expensive than Robusta beans. Hence, customers should prefer Cafe Mocha's coffee.

Question Stem:

Which of the following most accurately describes a flaw in the Cafe Mocha's argument?

Answer Choices:

A.) It assumes that Arabica beans are superior to Robusta beans just because they are more expensive.
B.) It overlooks the possibility that customers might prefer the taste of Robusta beans.
C.) It fails to consider that customers may prefer other factors, such as the freshness of the coffee.
D.) All of the above.
E.) None of the above.

* * *

Stimulus #18:

All Alpha Corporation employees are required to complete a six-month training program. Lisa just started working at Alpha Corporation.

Question Stem:

If the statements above are true, which of the following must also be true?

Answer Choices:

A.) Lisa will need to complete the six-month training program.
B.) Lisa has already completed the six-month training program.
C.) The six-month training program at Alpha Corporation is intensive.
D.) Lisa will not be able to perform her job duties until after she has completed the six-month training program.
E.) The six-month training program at Alpha Corporation is beneficial.

* * *

Stimulus #19:

During a medical conference, Dr. Adams argues that since all his patients who used a certain type of sunscreen experienced no sunburns, this type of sunscreen is perfect for preventing sunburns.

Question Stem:

Which of the following arguments is most similar in its reasoning to Dr. Adams's argument?

Answer Choices:

A.) John believes his sports team wins whenever he wears his lucky socks. Hence, his socks are the reason behind the team's success.
B.) A gardener found that her plants grew better when she played classical music to them. Therefore, all plants should be exposed to classical music to improve their growth.
C.) The city council states that because the crime rate dropped after installing more streetlights, streetlights deter crime.
D.) The chef claims that since none of his customers complained about the food, his restaurant serves the best food in town.
E.) The teacher thinks that because her students perform well on tests, her teaching methods are the most effective.

***

Stimulus #20:

Jane argues that we should stop using paper cups because producing them contributes to deforestation. Instead, she suggests that everyone should use reusable cups.

Question Stem:

Which of the following, if true, would most weaken Jane's argument?

Answer Choices:

A.) Paper cups can be recycled.
B.) Reusable cups require a significant amount of energy to produce.
C.) Deforestation is a leading cause of global warming.
D.) Many coffee shops offer discounts to customers who bring their reusable cups.
E.) Using reusable cups can reduce waste in landfills.

***

Stimulus #21:

A recent poll found that 80% of people who frequently consume energy drinks report feeling more alert. Therefore, energy drinks are effective at increasing alertness.

Question Stem:

Which one of the following describes a flaw in the reasoning above?

Answer Choices:

A.) The argument incorrectly equates correlation with causation.
B.) The argument is based on a biased sample.
C.) The argument fails to consider the potential negative effects of energy drinks.
D.) The argument relies on an appeal to popularity.
E.) The argument does not provide a clear definition of what constitutes "alertness."

***

Stimulus #22:

During a meeting, the city council decided to pass a law to prohibit the use of cell phones while crossing streets. This action was taken to minimize pedestrian accidents.

Question Stem:

Which one of the following principles, if valid, would most help to justify the city council's decision?

Answer Choices:

A.) Laws should be created to regulate every aspect of people's lives.
B.) Public safety should be a priority, even if it requires limiting certain individual freedoms.
C.) The freedom to use a cell phone whenever and wherever one wishes is a fundamental right.
D.) Pedestrian accidents are the leading cause of death in urban areas.
E.) Cell phones are unnecessary distractions and should be eliminated.

***

Stimulus #23:

While the government was unsuccessful in their bid to reduce greenhouse gas emissions last year, they have implemented new policies this year aimed at targeting major industrial contributors. If these policies are enforced and adhered to, the emission levels will certainly be reduced.

Question Stem:

If all the statements above are true, which one of the following must also be true?

Answer Choices:

A.) The government's policies from last year were not targeting major industrial contributors.
B.) Major industrial contributors are the primary source of greenhouse gas emissions.
C.) The new policies will be successful in reducing greenhouse gas emissions.
D.) The new policies are better than the policies from the previous year.
E.) The government failed to enforce the policies last year.

* * *

Stimulus #24:

Just as a gardener must remove weeds for flowers to flourish, so too must a teacher eliminate distractions in the classroom to promote effective learning.

Question Stem:

Which one of the following arguments is most similar in its reasoning to the argument above?

Answer Choices:

A.) To make a delicious soup, the chef must use fresh ingredients, just as a painter needs quality paints to create a good painting.
B.) Like a conductor leading an orchestra to create harmonious music, a project manager must coordinate a team to accomplish a project successfully.
C.) An athlete needs to follow a rigorous training routine to excel, just as a pilot needs rigorous training to fly a plane.
D.) Just as a mechanic needs to remove faulty parts from a car for it to run well, a doctor must remove unhealthy tissues for a patient to recover.
E.) A well-trained dog obeys its master's commands just like a well-programmed computer executes commands.

* * *

Stimulus #25:

In a survey conducted among university students, it was found that those who played sports had a significantly higher grade point average (GPA) than those who didn't. Hence, playing sports increases academic performance.

Question Stem:

Which one of the following, if true, most seriously weakens the argument?

Answer Choices:

A.) The students who played sports also reported having better time management skills than those who did not play sports.
B.) The survey was conducted only in one university, not nationwide.
C.) There are some students who do not play sports but still have high GPAs.
D.) The students who played sports also reported getting more sleep on average than those who did not play sports.
E.) The majority of the students surveyed did not play sports.

9

Practice Exercise 1: Answers & Explanations

Stimulus #1:

Correct Answer:

Choice E. The study did not account for dietary habits and other lifestyle factors.

Correct Answer Explanation:

The argument states that regular physical exercise lowers the risk of developing heart disease. To weaken this argument, we need to find an answer choice that introduces doubt or casts doubt on the relationship between exercise and heart disease. Choice E is the correct answer because it points out that the study did not consider other factors, such as dietary habits and lifestyle choices, that could potentially influence the development of heart disease. By failing to account for these factors, the study's conclusion may be incomplete or overstated.

Explanation for Incorrect Choices:

Choice A. Most heart disease cases are primarily caused by genetic factors is incorrect because it does not weaken the argument. The argument is focused on the benefits of exercise, not the causes of heart disease.

Choice B. The study did not differentiate between different types of physical exercise is incorrect because it is not the most serious weakening option. While it raises a potential limitation of the study, it does not directly challenge the conclusion that regular exercise is crucial for maintaining a healthy heart.

Choice C. Individuals who engage in physical exercise have a higher likelihood of developing other health problems is incorrect because it is irrelevant to the argument. The argument is concerned with the risk of heart disease, not other health problems.

Choice D. The study only considered individuals between the ages of 20 and 30 is incorrect because it does not significantly weaken the argument. The age restriction might limit the applicability of the study's findings, but it does not directly challenge the conclusion that regular exercise is beneficial for heart health.

Stimulus #2:

Correct Answer:

Choice A. Socrates is a thinker.

Correct Answer Explanation:

The premises of the argument are as follows: "All philosophers are thinkers" and "Socrates is a philosopher." From these premises, the most strongly supported conclusion is "Socrates is a thinker" (Answer Choice A). This conclusion essentially restates the second premise, with "thinker" replacing "philosopher," based on the relationship established in the first premise.

Explanation for Incorrect Choices:

Choice B. All thinkers are philosophers. This statement is incorrect. The stimulus tells us that all philosophers are thinkers, but it doesn't state that all thinkers are philosophers.

Choice C. Socrates is not a thinker. This contradicts the logical conclusion derived from the stimulus, which is that Socrates is a thinker.

Choice D. Socrates could be a musician. The stimulus does not provide any information about Socrates being a musician, making this choice incorrect.

Choice E. All philosophers are Socrates. The stimulus states that Socrates is a philosopher, but it does not suggest that all philosophers are Socrates, making this choice incorrect as well.

***

Stimulus #3:

Correct Answer:

Choice A. If Lisa is not a member of the soccer team, then Lisa did not attend the meeting.

Correct Answer Explanation:

The given premises are: "Every member of the soccer team attended the meeting" and "If Lisa attended the meeting, then Lisa is a member of the soccer team." From these premises, the conclusion that most directly follows is: "If Lisa is not a member of the soccer team, then Lisa did not attend the meeting" (Answer Choice A). This conclusion represents the contrapositive of the second premise. In logic, when a statement takes the form "If P, then Q," its contrapositive is "If not Q, then not P." Therefore, if it is true that Lisa attending the meeting implies her membership in the team, it is also true that if Lisa is not a team member, she did not attend the meeting.

Explanation for Incorrect Choices:

Choice B. Every member of the soccer team is named Lisa. This is incorrect. The stimulus only indicates that if Lisa attended the meeting, she's a member of the team. It doesn't suggest that all team members are named Lisa.

Choice C. Lisa is the only member of the soccer team. This is incorrect. The stimulus doesn't state that Lisa is the only member of the team, only that if she attended the meeting, she's a member of the team.

Choice D. If Lisa did not attend the meeting, she is not a member of the soccer team. This is incorrect. The stimulus does not provide information to support this conclusion. It's possible for Lisa to be a team member and have missed the meeting.

Choice E. If you are not Lisa, then you are not a member of the soccer team. This is incorrect. The stimulus does not suggest that only Lisa can be a member of the soccer team. Other people can also be members.

***

Stimulus #4:

Correct Answer:

Choice A. It did not continue to rain.

Correct Answer Explanation:

The premises in the stimulus were "If the rain continues, the game will be postponed" and "The game was not postponed." In propositional logic, if we have a statement of the form "If P then Q," and we know that "Not Q" is true, we can conclude "Not P." This is a valid argument form known as modus tollens. So, since the game was not postponed (Not Q), we can conclude that it did not continue to rain (Not P).

Explanation for Incorrect Choices:

Choice B. The game was held in the rain. This is incorrect because we don't have information that confirms whether the game was held in the rain. We only know that it did not continue to rain.

Choice C. The rain stopped before the game. This statement is incorrect. The stimulus doesn't provide information about when the rain stopped. All we know is that it didn't continue to rain.

Choice D. The game was canceled. This is incorrect. The stimulus explicitly mentions that the game was not postponed, but there is no information about it being canceled.

Choice E. It was sunny during the game. This is incorrect because we don't have information about the weather during the game. The stimulus doesn't mention anything about sunshine.

* * *

Stimulus #5:

Correct Answer:

Choice A. Some creative people are not patient.

Correct Answer Explanation:

The premises in the stimulus were "All novelists are creative" and "Some novelists are not patient." From the first premise, we know that if someone is a novelist, they are creative. The second premise tells us that there are some novelists who are not patient. So, given that these not-patient individuals are also novelists, and therefore creative, we can conclude that there are some creative individuals who are not patient.

Explanation for Incorrect Choices:

Choice B. All patient people are novelists. This is incorrect. The stimulus doesn't state that all patient people are novelists. It only mentions that some novelists are not patient.

Choice C. All creative people are novelists. This is incorrect. The stimulus states that all novelists are creative, but it doesn't state that all creative people are novelists.

Choice D. Some patient people are not creative. This is incorrect. The stimulus does not provide information that supports this conclusion.

Choice E. No patient person is creative. This is incorrect. The stimulus states that some novelists (who are creative) are not patient. It doesn't say anything about patient people not being creative.

***

Stimulus #6:

Correct Answer:

Choice B. Sarah works in Accounting.

Correct Answer Explanation:

The stimulus provides that "Every employee at the firm works either in Accounting or in Marketing" and "No one in Marketing works on weekends." Since Sarah works on weekends, it can be inferred that she must work in Accounting because Marketing is excluded by the given conditions.

Explanation for Incorrect Choices:

Choice A. Sarah works in Marketing. This is incorrect. The stimulus clearly states that no one in Marketing works on weekends, and since Sarah works on weekends, she cannot be in Marketing.

Choice C. Sarah does not work at the firm. This is incorrect. The stimulus doesn't provide enough information to reach this conclusion. Given that Sarah works on weekends and all employees at the firm work either in Accounting or Marketing, it's reasonable to infer that Sarah works at the firm, in Accounting.

Choice D. Everyone who works on weekends is in Accounting. This is incorrect. While we know that Sarah, who works on weekends, is in Accounting, we don't know whether this is true of all weekend workers.

Choice E. No one in Accounting works on weekends. This is incorrect. We know that Sarah works on weekends and is in Accounting, so it's not true that no one in Accounting works on weekends.

***

Stimulus #7:

Correct Answer:

Choice E. No trees are animals.

Correct Answer Explanation:

Based on the given premises, we know "All cats are animals," "No plants are animals," and "Some trees are plants." This implies that since trees fall into the category of plants (even if not all trees are plants, some are), and no plants are animals, no trees could be animals either. Therefore, the answer choice "E. No trees are animals" is correct.

Explanation for Incorrect Choices:

Choice A. Some trees are cats. This is incorrect. While the stimulus mentions that all cats are animals and some trees are plants, there's no established link between cats and trees.

Choice B. No cats are trees. This is incorrect. Even though it seems plausible given the premises, it doesn't directly follow from the given statements. There's no stated relationship between cats and trees.

Choice C. Some plants are cats. This is incorrect. The stimulus states that no plants are animals and that all cats are animals, which means that no plants can be cats.

Choice D. All animals are trees. This is incorrect. There's no evidence in the stimulus that suggests all animals are trees.

* * *

Stimulus #8:

Correct Answer:

Choice B. Jackson worked 40 hours or less last week.

Correct Answer Explanation:

According to the company policy, an employee will receive overtime pay if they work more than 40 hours in a week. Jackson did not receive overtime pay last week, so it's safe to infer that he worked 40 hours or less.

Explanation for Incorrect Choices:

Choice A. Jackson is not an employee of the company. This is incorrect. There's not enough information to infer Jackson's employment status at the company.

Choice C. Jackson worked more than 40 hours last week. This is incorrect. If Jackson had worked more than 40 hours, he should have received overtime pay according to company policy.

Choice D. Jackson received less pay than he should have. This is incorrect. There's no information to suggest that Jackson was underpaid. The lack of overtime pay simply suggests he didn't exceed the 40-hour threshold.

Choice E. The company policy does not apply to Jackson. This is incorrect. There's no information to suggest that Jackson is exempt from the company policy.

* * *

Stimulus #9:

Correct Answer:

Choice E. Some red things are roses.

Correct Answer Explanation:

The stimulus states that all roses are flowers and some flowers are red, but doesn't provide a direct link between roses and red. The conclusion "some roses are red" is based on this indirect link. If we know that some red things are roses, this would directly strengthen the argument.

Explanation for Incorrect Choices:

Choice A. Some roses are not red. This is incorrect. Stating that some roses are not red does not strengthen the claim that some roses are red.

Choice B. All roses are red. This is incorrect. While it might seem like this strengthens the argument, the original argument is about some (not all) roses being red.

Choice C. All red things are flowers. This is incorrect. The claim isn't about all red things but about some roses.

Choice D. Some flowers are not red. This is incorrect. This statement does not add any strength to the argument that some roses are red.

* * *

Stimulus #10:

Correct Answer:

Choice E. John may live in the Southside district.

Correct Answer Explanation:

The information in the stimulus only establishes that John, a resident of Town X, was a victim of a crime last year. While the Northside district has a higher crime rate, it doesn't necessarily mean that John lives there. He could be a victim of crime in the Southside district as well.

Explanation for Incorrect Choices:

Choice A. John lives in the Northside district. This is incorrect. While the Northside district has a higher crime rate, it doesn't necessarily mean that John lives there. He could be a victim of crime in the Southside district as well.

Choice B. Crime rates in Town X are higher than average. This is incorrect. The stimulus does not provide any information about average crime rates, so we cannot make this inference.

Choice C. John is more likely to be a victim of a crime this year. This is incorrect. The stimulus does not provide any information about the likelihood of John being a victim of a crime this year.

Choice D. John was a victim of two crimes last year. This is incorrect. The fact that the Northside district had twice the crime rate of the Southside district does not imply that John was a victim of two crimes.

* * *

Stimulus #11:

Correct Answer:

Choice E. Some non-aggressive animals are dogs.

Correct Answer Explanation:

The stimulus provides that all dogs bark and some animals that bark are not aggressive, leading to the conclusion that some dogs are not aggressive. If we know that some non-aggressive animals are dogs, this would directly strengthen the argument that some dogs are not aggressive.

Explanation for Incorrect Choices:

Choice A. Some aggressive animals do not bark. This is incorrect. It doesn't have any bearing on the argument about dogs, barking, and aggression.

Choice B. All dogs are animals. This is incorrect. While it is a true statement, it doesn't add to the argument about some dogs not being aggressive.

Choice C. All animals that bark are dogs. This is incorrect. Even if true, it wouldn't strengthen the argument that some dogs are not aggressive.

Choice D. Some dogs are aggressive. This is incorrect. This would not strengthen the argument. It's unrelated to the claim about some dogs not being aggressive.

***

Stimulus #12:

Correct Answer:

Choice B. Rainfall in City A is more intense when it does rain.

Correct Answer Explanation:

The statements indicate that City A has a higher average rainfall per year but fewer rainy days than City B. This suggests that, on average, City A gets more rainfall per rainy day, which can be interpreted as the rain being more intense when it does rain in City A.

Explanation for Incorrect Choices:

Choice A. Rainfall in City B is more evenly distributed throughout the year. This is incorrect. The stimulus does not provide enough information about the distribution of rainfall throughout the year.

Choice C. City B had a wetter year than City A last year. This is incorrect. More rainy days in City B do not necessarily mean that it had more total rainfall.

Choice D. The climate in City B is wetter than in City A. This is incorrect. The number of rainy days does not necessarily reflect the overall wetness of the climate.

Choice E. City A will have more rainy days than City B this year. This is incorrect. The information given does not provide any basis for predicting future rainfall patterns.

* * *

Stimulus #13:

Correct Answer:

Choice A. Sam does not consume enough carbohydrates.

Correct Answer Explanation:

The argument is based on the assumption that because Sam, an athlete, eats plenty of protein, he is maintaining a healthy diet. But if Sam doesn't consume enough carbohydrates, another key component of a balanced diet, then this weakens the argument that Sam is maintaining a healthy diet, even if he consumes sufficient protein.

Explanation for Incorrect Choices:

Choice B. Sam has won several sports competitions. This is incorrect. Winning sports competitions doesn't necessarily mean Sam is maintaining a healthy diet. Athletic performance can be influenced by a variety of factors.

Choice C. Sam takes protein supplements daily. This is incorrect. This would further support, not weaken, the argument that Sam maintains a healthy diet (given the argument's focus on protein).

Choice D. Sam is considered one of the best athletes in his school. This is incorrect. Being considered a good athlete does not necessarily equate to maintaining a healthy diet.

Choice E. Sam also includes fruits and vegetables in his diet. This is incorrect. Including fruits and vegetables in one's diet typically indicate a healthy diet, so this statement would likely strengthen, not weaken the argument.

* * *

Stimulus #14:

Correct Answer:

Choice D. Jane is more likely to become a successful businessperson than before she subscribed to the financial news.

Correct Answer Explanation:

Jane taking an action that is associated with successful businesspeople (reading daily financial news) may increase her chances of becoming a successful businessperson. However, this does not guarantee success, nor does it establish that Jane subscribed to the news for this specific reason.

Explanation for Incorrect Choices:

Choice A. Reading the daily financial news will make Jane a successful businessperson. This is incorrect. The stimulus suggests that reading daily financial news is a habit of successful businesspeople, but it doesn't prove causation, i.e., that reading such news will necessarily make Jane successful.

Choice B. Jane will become a successful businessperson. This is incorrect. While Jane is taking steps in the right direction, there is no certainty she will become successful.

Choice C. Jane is a successful businessperson. This is incorrect. The stimulus only tells us that Jane wants to be successful, not that she already is.

Choice E. Jane subscribed to the financial news because most successful businesspeople do. This is incorrect. The stimulus does not specify the reason why Jane decided to subscribe to the financial news.

***

Stimulus #15:

Correct Answer:

Choice B. All fruits are not vegetables.

Correct Answer Explanation:

This answer directly strengthens the argument that no apples are vegetables, as apples are categorized as fruits. If all fruits are not vegetables, then apples, being fruits, cannot be vegetables. The color of apples or vegetables, or the general characteristics of green things, do not strengthen this specific argument.

Explanation for Incorrect Choices:

Choice A. Some vegetables are green. This is incorrect. The color of vegetables does not strengthen the argument about the categorization of apples.

Choice C. Some apples are red. This is incorrect. The color of apples doesn't have any bearing on whether they are vegetables or not.

Choice D. No fruits are green. This is incorrect. The color of fruits doesn't strengthen the argument about whether apples are vegetables or not.

Choice E. All green things are vegetables. This is incorrect. The color of things being related to them being vegetables does not contribute to the argument about apples.

***

Stimulus #16:

Correct Answer:

Choice D. Charles has a greater chance of winning the Pulitzer Prize for Fiction than a writer who has not studied literature at a university or written critically acclaimed stories.

Correct Answer Explanation:

Charles likely has a greater chance of winning than a writer without these experiences.

Explanation for Incorrect Choices:

Choice A. Charles will win the Pulitzer Prize for Fiction. This is incorrect. The information does not guarantee Charles will win the Pulitzer Prize for Fiction.

Choice B. Charles' novel will be a bestseller. This is incorrect. The information does not provide a basis for predicting sales of Charles' novel.

Choice C. Charles is likely to become a professor of literature at a university. This is incorrect. There's no information suggesting Charles is likely to become a literature professor.

Choice E. Charles will write another novel. This is incorrect. The stimulus does not provide information regarding Charles' future writing plans.

* * *

Stimulus #17:

Correct Answer:

Choice A. John's athletic profession requires him to train rigorously every day.

Correct Answer Explanation:

This answer weakens the argument by suggesting that John's rigorous daily training may counteract the obesity risk associated with frequent fast food consumption.

Explanation for Incorrect Choices:

Choice B. John prefers fast food to home-cooked meals. This is incorrect. John's preference for fast food does not directly influence his likelihood of developing obesity.

Choice C. People who exercise regularly can still develop obesity. This is incorrect. This statement could suggest that John is still at risk despite his profession, so it does not weaken the argument.

Choice D. The study did not consider the lifestyle or physical activity levels of the subjects. This is incorrect. While true, this information does not specifically relate to John's circumstances as an athlete who trains rigorously daily.

Choice E. Fast food is a major contributor to the global obesity epidemic. This is incorrect. This statement strengthens, rather than weakens, the argument about the correlation between fast food and obesity.

***

Stimulus #18:

Correct Answer:

Choice D. Claire is likely to have more advanced cognitive skills and better problem-solving abilities compared to some monolingual children her age.

Correct Answer Explanation:

Given that Claire is growing up in a bilingual environment, it is likely, based on the studies, that she may have more advanced cognitive skills and problem-solving abilities compared to some monolingual children her age.

Explanation for Incorrect Choices:

Choice A. Claire will outperform all her peers in cognitive tasks. This is incorrect. While the statement suggests that Claire might have advanced cognitive skills, it does not imply that she will outperform ALL her peers.

Choice B. Claire will become a translator when she grows up. This is incorrect. The stimulus does not provide any information about Claire's future career.

Choice C. All bilingual children are smarter than monolingual children. This is incorrect. The stimulus does not suggest that ALL bilingual children are smarter, just that they may have some cognitive advantages.

Choice E. Claire's parents are language teachers. This is incorrect. There's no information suggesting that Claire's parents are language teachers.

***

Stimulus #19:

Correct Answer:

Choice E. A significant portion of Boston's population prefers driving over using public transportation.

Correct Answer Explanation:

This statement suggests that despite the extensive public transportation system, many people in Boston prefer to drive. This could explain why Boston's obesity rates are high despite the city's extensive public transportation system.

Explanation for Incorrect Choices:

Choice A. Boston's public transportation system has been facing frequent service disruptions recently. This is incorrect. Service disruptions could potentially decrease public transportation use, but this doesn't directly explain the surge in obesity rates.

Choice B. Most cities with low rates of obesity have a well-established healthcare system. This is incorrect. This information about healthcare systems is not relevant to the correlation between public transportation use and obesity rates.

Choice C. Boston has the largest public transportation system in the country. This is incorrect. The size of the public transportation system doesn't necessarily correlate with its use or with obesity rates.

Choice D. Obesity rates are generally higher in cities with colder climates. This is incorrect. While this might explain higher obesity rates, it doesn't address the high public transportation availability paradox with increased obesity.

***

Stimulus #20:

Correct Answer:

Choice C. Company Z's customer loyalty program is very complex and difficult to understand.

Correct Answer Explanation:

If the customer loyalty program is too complex to understand, customers might be discouraged from making purchases, hence explaining the decrease in sales.

Explanation for Incorrect Choices:

Choice A. Many customers of Company Z made bulk purchases before the implementation of the loyalty program. This is incorrect. While this might explain a temporary dip in sales after the bulk purchases, it doesn't explain why sales didn't increase with the loyalty program.

Choice B. Company Z's competitors do not offer any customer loyalty programs. This is incorrect. What Company Z's competitors do or don't do doesn't address the paradox in Company Z's sales.

Choice D. The products offered by Company Z are of high quality. This is incorrect. The quality of products is not relevant in explaining the paradox related to the impact of the loyalty program on sales.

Choice E. Some customers of Company Z do not make purchases frequently. This is incorrect. While infrequent purchases by some customers could contribute to lower sales, it doesn't explain the impact of the new loyalty program.

***

Stimulus #21:

Correct Answer:

Choice D. Exposure to art at a young age can influence a child's appreciation of art.

Correct Answer Explanation:

The argument assumes that early exposure to art can influence a child's appreciation of it, which is why the curriculum should include museum visits.

Explanation for Incorrect Choices:

Choice A. All children will develop a love for art if exposed to artworks at a young age. This is incorrect. The argument doesn't assume that all children will develop a love for art, just that exposure can foster this love.

Choice B. Art museums are the only places where children can be exposed to artworks. This is incorrect. The argument doesn't suggest that art museums are the only places for this exposure.

Choice C. Regular visits to art museums will guarantee a love for art in all children. This is incorrect. The argument doesn't claim that regular visits will guarantee a love for art, only that they can foster it.

Choice E. School curricula currently lack sufficient exposure to art. This is incorrect. The current state of school curricula is not assumed in the argument. The argument is suggesting an addition, not claiming a deficiency.

* * *

Stimulus #22:

Correct Answer:

Choice B. The majority of students in School Y, who eat in the cafeteria, complain about stomachaches. Therefore, the cafeteria food is probably causing the stomachaches.

Correct Answer Explanation:

This argument mirrors the original argument by linking complaints (stomachaches or air pollution) from a group of people (students or residents) to a probable cause (cafeteria food or the old factory).

Explanation for Incorrect Choices:

Choice A. Many people who enjoy playing sports also follow sports news, so playing sports causes interest in sports news. This is incorrect. The connection between enjoying and following sports is not a cause-effect relationship as in the original argument.

Choice C. As many people who live in City Z complain about traffic, there must be a lot of cars in City Z. This is incorrect. This argument assumes a cause-effect relationship between complaints and traffic, which is different from the original argument.

Choice D. Many residents of City W, who work in the downtown area, complain about noise pollution. Therefore, the downtown area is too noisy. This is incorrect. This argument concludes on the state (noisiness) of the downtown area, not its causality, unlike the original argument.

Choice E. Most visitors to Park K, who picnic near the lake, complain about mosquitoes. Hence, the lake is infested with mosquitoes. This is incorrect. While this argument presents a similar structure, it incorrectly identifies a symptom (mosquitoes) as the cause, unlike the original argument.

＊＊＊

Stimulus #23:

Correct Answer:

Choice A. Everything that belongs to a certain category shares all the features of that category.

Correct Answer Explanation:

John's argument is based on the principle that if something is a part of a certain group, it shares the attributes of that group. In this case, being a fruit means being a good source of vitamins.

Explanation for Incorrect Choices:

Choice B. Apples are the best source of vitamins among all fruits. This is incorrect. John's argument doesn't require apples to be the best source of vitamins, just a good one.

Choice C. If something is a good source of vitamins, it must be a fruit. This is incorrect. John's argument doesn't assume that all good sources of vitamins are fruits, only that fruits (like apples) are good sources.

Choice D. Only fruits are good sources of vitamins. This is incorrect. The argument doesn't rely on the principle that only fruits are good sources of vitamins.

Choice E. Fruits that are not good sources of vitamins are not truly fruits. This is incorrect. John's argument doesn't rely on redefining what constitutes a fruit based on vitamin content.

* * *

Stimulus #24:

Correct Answer:

Choice C. Many regular theater-goers have expressed disappointment with the recent performances of the local theater company.

Correct Answer Explanation:

If regular theater-goers are disappointed with the company's recent performances, they may be less likely to attend upcoming plays, thus strengthening the argument.

Explanation for Incorrect Choices:

Choice A. The local theater company has been around for more than 20 years. This is incorrect. The company's long history does not necessarily influence the attendance of future plays.

Choice B. The play being staged next month is written by a very popular and acclaimed playwright. This is incorrect. This would potentially weaken the argument as it suggests the upcoming play might draw a larger audience due to the popularity of the playwright.

Choice D. The theater where the play will be staged has been recently renovated. This is incorrect. A renovated theater could potentially attract more attendees, thus weakening the argument.

Choice E. The theater company has a new director with an innovative approach to staging plays. This is incorrect. A new, innovative director might attract more audience, which would weaken the argument.

* * *

Stimulus #25:

Correct Answer:

Choice C. The drivers in Country X are required to undergo a rigorous driving test before obtaining their licenses.

Correct Answer Explanation:

If drivers in Country X undergo rigorous driving tests, they could be better prepared and safer on the road, leading to fewer accidents despite the higher number of vehicles.

Explanation for Incorrect Choices:

Choice A. Country X has more urban areas than Country Y. This is incorrect. More urban areas could potentially lead to more traffic accidents due to higher vehicle density.

Choice B. The population of Country Y is significantly smaller than that of Country X. This is incorrect. A smaller population in Country Y doesn't explain why it would have more traffic accidents if there are fewer vehicles.

Choice D. Country X has a significantly larger land area than Country Y. This is incorrect. A larger land area could potentially spread vehicles out more, but this doesn't necessarily correlate with fewer traffic accidents.

Choice E. Country Y has a higher percentage of elderly drivers than Country X. This is incorrect. A higher percentage of elderly drivers in Country Y doesn't necessarily lead to more accidents. Moreover, it could be argued that older drivers might drive less frequently, reducing the potential for accidents.

***

10
Practice Exercise 2: Answers & Explanations

Stimulus #1:

Correct Answer:

Choice A. I always get a headache when I study for too long. I studied for five hours yesterday and now I have a headache. Therefore, studying for long hours is the cause of my headache.

Correct Answer Explanation:

This argument follows the same structure as the original: X happens whenever I do Y. I did Y, and X happened. Therefore, Y causes X.

Explanation for Incorrect Choices:

Choice B. Every time it rains, my car won't start. It rained yesterday and my car won't start today. Therefore, the rain causes my car's engine to malfunction. This is incorrect. While this argument is similar, it introduces a new concept (engine malfunction) that isn't directly equivalent to the original argument's reasoning.

Choice C. I always get a fever when I catch a cold. I have a fever today, so I must have a cold. This is incorrect. This argument infers that the presence of one condition (a fever) necessarily indicates another condition (a cold), which is different from the original argument's reasoning.

Choice D. Whenever I drink coffee, I feel more alert. I drank coffee this morning and I feel alert. Therefore, coffee is a stimulant. This is incorrect. This argument is a general assertion about coffee's effects, not a specific instance of cause and effect.

Choice E. Every time I eat spicy food, I get heartburn. I ate spicy food yesterday and today I don't have heartburn. Therefore, spicy food isn't the cause of my heartburn. This is incorrect. This argument presents a contradiction to the established pattern, unlike the original argument.

***

Stimulus #2:

Correct Answer:

Choice D. It assumes that an increase in the number of passengers means an increase in satisfaction.

Correct Answer Explanation

The main flaw in the argument is the assumption that if more people are using the service, they must be satisfied with it, which isn't necessarily true.

Explanation for Incorrect Choices:

Choice A. It fails to consider that the increase in passengers might be due to factors other than the quality of the service. This is incorrect. Although true, this doesn't describe the primary flaw in the argument, which is assuming increased usage equals increased satisfaction.

Choice B. It assumes that all passengers have the same standards for public transportation. This is incorrect. The argument does not make any assumptions about the standards of the passengers.

Choice C. It fails to provide evidence that complaints have decreased as the number of passengers increased. This is incorrect. While true, this is not the main flaw in the argument. The argument is flawed because it assumes more usage equates to fewer valid complaints.

Choice E. It fails to consider that more passengers might lead to more complaints. This is incorrect. While this might be a valid point, it doesn't address the fundamental flaw in the argument, which is the assumption that increased usage implies satisfaction or invalidates complaints.

* * *

Stimulus #3:

Correct Answer:

Choice D. There are no exceptions to the graduation requirement of completing a mathematics course.

Correct Answer Explanation:

The argument assumes that the requirement applies to all students, with no exceptions.

Explanation for Incorrect Choices:

Choice A. John wants to graduate. This is incorrect. The argument does not rely on John's desire to graduate.

Choice B. John has not yet completed a mathematics course. This is incorrect. The argument doesn't assume this; John's status regarding the course is not mentioned or assumed.

Choice C. Every university student must take the same mathematics course. This is incorrect. The type of mathematics course is not mentioned or assumed in the argument.

Choice E. John is incapable of completing a mathematics course. This is incorrect. The argument doesn't assume anything about John's capability to complete the course.

***

Stimulus #4:

Correct Answer:

Choice C. Susan is eligible for the loyalty bonus.

Correct Answer Explanation:

Given the facts, we can infer that Susan, having worked at the company for 7 years, is eligible for the loyalty bonus.

Explanation for Incorrect Choices:

Choice A. Susan has received the loyalty bonus. This is incorrect. While Susan is eligible for the bonus, it does not guarantee she has received it.

Choice B. Susan is not eligible for the loyalty bonus. This is incorrect. The facts clearly state that Susan is eligible for the bonus.

Choice D. All employees who have worked for the company for more than 5 years receive the loyalty bonus. This is incorrect. While the eligibility criterion is met for employees with over 5 years of service, there is no guarantee that they receive the bonus.

Choice E. Susan has been with the company longer than any other employee. This is incorrect. There is no information given about the tenure of other employees.

***

Stimulus #5:

Correct Answer:

Choice D. No chairs are comfortable because all chairs are furniture, and all furniture is uncomfortable.

Correct Answer Explanation:

This follows the same structure: No X are Y because all X are Z, and all Z are Y.

Explanation for Incorrect Choices:

Choice A. All mammals are warm-blooded, and all cats are mammals. Therefore, all cats are warm-blooded. This is incorrect. This example illustrates transitive property, not parallel reasoning.

Choice B. No cars are cheap because all cars are machines, and all machines are expensive. This is incorrect. This isn't parallel because it incorrectly implies that all machines (not just cars) are expensive.

Choice C. All dogs are animals, and all animals need food. Therefore, all dogs need food. This is incorrect. This example illustrates transitive property, not parallel reasoning.

Choice E. All fish live in water, and all sharks are fish. Therefore, all sharks live in water. This is incorrect. This example illustrates transitive property, not parallel reasoning.

***

Stimulus #6:

Correct Answer:

Choice E. All of the above.

Correct Answer Explanation:

All of the above flaws are present in the argument. This is the correct answer.

Explanation for Incorrect Choices:

Choice A. The argument presumes, without providing justification, that the only purpose of the law was to affect crime rates. This is correct. The argument presumes without justification that the law's only purpose was to affect crime rates. While this answer is correct, the actual answer is Choice E.

Choice B. The argument fails to consider that crime rates may have risen if the law had not been enacted. This is correct. The argument fails to consider that crime rates may have risen if the law had not been enacted. While this answer is correct, the actual answer is Choice E.

Choice C. The argument assumes that the new law should have had an immediate impact on crime rates. This is correct. The argument assumes that the law should have had an immediate impact on crime rates. While this answer is correct, the actual answer is Choice E.

Choice D. The argument overlooks the possibility that the law may have other benefits that are not related to crime rates. This is correct. The argument overlooks the possibility that the law may have benefits unrelated to crime rates. While this answer is correct, the actual answer is Choice E.

***

Stimulus #7:

Correct Answer:

Choice C. E-commerce is the future of shopping.

Correct Answer Explanation:

This is the point at issue. John believes that e-commerce is the future of shopping, whereas Sara disagrees, pointing to the enduring appeal of physical shopping.

Explanation for Incorrect Choices:

Choice A. The Internet is convenient for shopping. This is incorrect. Both John and Sara agree that the Internet is convenient for shopping.

Choice B. Physical shopping provides immediate gratification. This is incorrect. Both John and Sara agree that physical shopping provides immediate gratification.

Choice D. People prefer the tangible experience of physical shopping. This is incorrect. John does not necessarily disagree that people prefer the tangible experience of physical shopping.

Choice E. E-commerce and physical shopping can coexist. This is incorrect. The coexistence of e-commerce and physical shopping isn't directly discussed by either John or Sara.

***

Stimulus #8:

Correct Answer:

Choice A. Mary didn't study for the exam.

Correct Answer Explanation:

If studying leads to passing and Mary didn't pass, we can infer that she didn't study.

Explanation for Incorrect Choices:

Choice B. Mary studied for the exam. This is incorrect. The given statements actually suggest the opposite: that Mary didn't study.

Choice C. The exam was too difficult. This is incorrect. The difficulty of the exam is not discussed in the statements.

Choice D. Mary never studies for exams. This is incorrect. The statements only provide information about this particular exam, not all exams.

Choice E. Mary is not good at exams. This is incorrect. The statements don't provide sufficient information to make a judgment about Mary's overall exam performance.

***

Stimulus #9:

Correct Answer:

Choice A. The path to success is paved with countless failures.

Correct Answer Explanation:

This principle directly supports Jack's belief by implying that failure is a stepping stone to success.

Explanation for Incorrect Choices:

Choice B. One's ability to handle success is indicative of their character. This is incorrect. This principle is about handling success, not failure.

Choice C. .Failure should be avoided at all costs to be successful. This is incorrect. This principle contradicts Jack's belief.

Choice D. Success comes to those who work the hardest. This is incorrect. This principle doesn't mention dealing with failure.

Choice E. Success and failure are unrelated. This is incorrect. This principle contradicts Jack's belief.

* * *

Stimulus #10:

Correct Answer:

Choice B. More than half of the apples fell from the tree.

Correct Answer Explanation:

If more than half of the apples fell, it could explain why there were more oranges than apples left.

Explanation for Incorrect Choices:

Choice A. The oranges were smaller than the apples. This is incorrect. The size of the fruits doesn't explain the paradox.

Choice C. The oranges were more tightly attached to the tree than the apples. This is incorrect. The attachment of the fruits doesn't directly solve the paradox, as the condition stated that half of both fruits fell.

Choice D. The apples and oranges were counted incorrectly the first time. This is incorrect. This doesn't resolve the paradox, but instead implies an error in the initial data.

Choice E. The tree produces more oranges in a year than apples. This is incorrect. The tree's annual production doesn't resolve the discrepancy between the initial and final counts.

***

Stimulus #11:

Correct Answer:

Choice A. Leonardo da Vinci was not a great artist of the Renaissance.

Correct Answer Explanation:

If all great artists of the Renaissance were patrons of the Medici and Leonardo was not, then according to this logic, he could not have been a great artist of the Renaissance.

Explanation for Incorrect Choices:

Choice B. The Medici family were the only patrons of great artists in the Renaissance. This is incorrect. The stimulus does not specify that the Medicis were the only patrons.

Choice C. Leonardo da Vinci received patronage from another family. This is incorrect. The stimulus does not provide information about Leonardo's other patrons.

Choice D. The Medici family did not appreciate Leonardo da Vinci's art. This is incorrect. The stimulus does not provide information about the Medicis' appreciation of Leonardo's art.

Choice E. Leonardo da Vinci was a great artist of the Renaissance. This is incorrect. As per the logic of the stimulus, Leonardo wasn't a great artist of the Renaissance.

* * *

Stimulus #12:

Correct Answer:

Choice A. If a book is a bestseller, then it is well-written. But a well-written book will not necessarily be a bestseller.

Correct Answer Explanation:

This mirrors the structure of the original argument: having one quality ensures another, but the reverse isn't necessarily true.

Explanation for Incorrect Choices:

Choice B. If a painting is famous, it must be old. However, not all old paintings are famous. This is incorrect. The characteristics in this option (fame and age) do not have the same relationship as those in the original argument.

Choice C. If a song is catchy, it will be popular. But not all popular songs are catchy. This is incorrect. Catchiness leading to popularity is not the same relationship as in the original argument.

Choice D. If a play is long, it must be boring. But not all long plays are boring. This is incorrect. The characteristics in this option (length and boringness) do not have the same relationship as those in the original argument.

Choice E. If a car is expensive, it must be luxurious. But not all luxurious cars are expensive. This is incorrect. The cost of a car and its luxury are not the same relationship as in the original argument.

* * *

Stimulus #13:

Correct Answer:

Choice A. The needs of the many outweigh the needs of the few.

Correct Answer Explanation:

This principle aligns with the original argument that policies should benefit the majority, not the minority.

Explanation for Incorrect Choices:

Choice B. Minority rights should be protected at all costs. This is incorrect. This principle would support, not undermine, the policy in question.

Choice C. Any policy that benefits some at the expense of others is unjust. This is incorrect. This principle doesn't distinguish between majority and minority; the original argument does.

Choice D. The majority is not always right. This is incorrect. The stimulus doesn't concern the rightness or wrongness of the majority, just their benefit.

Choice E. Policy should first do no harm. This is incorrect. This principle could be used to critique many policies, but it doesn't specifically address the issue of majority vs. minority benefit.

* * *

Stimulus #14:

Correct Answer:

Choice B. People who exercise regularly are more likely to engage in outdoor activities, where they are more exposed to cold viruses.

Correct Answer Explanation:

Jane taking an action that is associated with successful businesspeople (reading daily financial news) may increase her chances of becoming a successful businessperson. However, this does not guarantee success, nor does it establish that Jane subscribed to the news for this specific reason.

Explanation for Incorrect Choices:

Choice A. The study did not take into account the dietary habits of the subjects. This is incorrect. Dietary habits are not related to the apparent paradox in the stimulus.

Choice C. Regular exercise reduces stress levels. This is incorrect. Stress levels are not mentioned in the paradox.

Choice D. The study included only a small sample of people. This is incorrect. The size of the sample in the study does not help resolve the paradox.

Choice E. Not all people who exercise regularly maintain a balanced diet. This is incorrect. Diet is not part of the paradox presented in the stimulus.

***

Stimulus #15:

Correct Answer:

Choice C. The school was the primary source of high-sugar snacks for the students.

Correct Answer Explanation:

The argument assumes that by removing high-sugar snacks from school, it significantly decreases the students' overall sugar intake.

Explanation for Incorrect Choices:

Choice A. The students will not bring high-sugar snacks from home. This is incorrect. While it might help the argument, it's not necessary. Students might still bring snacks, but the school was not assumed to be the only source.

Choice B. The students do not prefer high-sugar snacks. This is incorrect. The argument doesn't depend on the student's preference for snacks but on their access to them.

Choice D. The students do not consume high-sugar snacks outside of school. This is incorrect. The argument is about the sugar intake of students at school, not outside.

Choice E. The school can effectively enforce the ban on high-sugar snacks. This is incorrect. While this might be true, it's not assumed in the argument. The argument is about the effect of the policy, not its enforcement.

***

Stimulus #16:

Correct Answer:

Choice B. People who listen to classical music also tend to engage in other activities known to increase intelligence, such as reading.

Correct Answer Explanation:

If people who listen to classical music engage in other activities that increase intelligence, it could be these other activities, not the music, causing the higher IQ scores.

Explanation for Incorrect Choices:

Choice A. IQ tests are not the only measure of intelligence. This is incorrect. While true, it does not specifically weaken the correlation proposed between classical music and IQ scores.

Choice C. Classical music is often played in environments that stimulate intellectual activity. This is incorrect. The environment is not addressed in the argument; it's about the direct influence of classical music on IQ scores.

Choice D. People who score higher on IQ tests also tend to earn more money. This is incorrect. The earning potential of high IQ individuals is irrelevant to the argument's concern with classical music and IQ scores.

Choice E. The majority of high IQ individuals reported that they prefer classical music over other genres. This is incorrect. This actually strengthens the argument rather than weakening it.

***

Stimulus #17:

Correct Answer:

Choice D. All of the above.

Correct Answer Explanation:

This captures all of the flaws present in the argument.

Explanation for Incorrect Choices:

Choice A. It assumes that Arabica beans are superior to Robusta beans just because they are more expensive. This is correct. The argument presumes that a higher price tag equates to higher quality, which is not necessarily true. While this answer is correct, the actual answer is Choice D.

Choice B. It overlooks the possibility that customers might prefer the taste of Robusta beans. This is correct. Taste is subjective, and some customers might prefer Robusta beans. While this answer is correct, the actual answer is Choice D.

Choice C. It fails to consider that customers may prefer other factors, such as the freshness of the coffee. This is correct. The argument does not consider other factors that could influence a customer's preference, like freshness. While this answer is correct, the actual answer is Choice D.

Choice E. None of the above. This is incorrect. There are various flaws in the argument.

* * *

Stimulus #18:

Correct Answer:

Choice A. Lisa will need to complete the six-month training program.

Correct Answer Explanation:

Given that all employees must complete the program and Lisa is an employee, it logically follows that Lisa must complete the program.

Explanation for Incorrect Choices:

Choice B. Lisa has already completed the six-month training program. This is incorrect. The stimulus only indicates that Lisa has started working, not that she has completed the training program.

Choice C. The six-month training program at Alpha Corporation is intensive. This is incorrect. The intensity of the training program is not discussed in the stimulus.

Choice D. Lisa will not be able to perform her job duties until after she has completed the six-month training program. This is incorrect. There's no evidence suggesting that Lisa can't perform any job duties until after training.

Choice E. The six-month training program at Alpha Corporation is beneficial. This is incorrect. Whether or not the training program is beneficial is not discussed in the stimulus.

＊＊＊

Stimulus #19:

Correct Answer:

Choice C. The city council states that because the crime rate dropped after installing more streetlights, streetlights deter crime.

Correct Answer Explanation:

Both Dr. Adams and the city council are attributing the prevention of a negative outcome (sunburns or crime) to a specific cause (sunscreen or streetlights).

Explanation for Incorrect Choices:

Choice A. John believes his sports team wins whenever he wears his lucky socks. Hence, his socks are the reason behind the team's success. This is incorrect. John's belief is based on superstition, not evidence.

Choice B. A gardener found that her plants grew better when she played classical music to them. Therefore, all plants should be exposed to classical music to improve their growth. This is incorrect. This argument involves the growth of plants, not the prevention of a negative outcome.

Choice D. The chef claims that since none of his customers complained about the food, his restaurant serves the best food in town. This is incorrect. The lack of complaints is not equivalent to a positive outcome, such as the prevention of sunburns.

Choice E. The teacher thinks that because her students perform well on tests, her teaching methods are the most effective. This is incorrect. The teacher's argument deals with improving performance, not preventing a negative outcome.

***

Stimulus #20:

Correct Answer:

Choice B. Reusable cups require a significant amount of energy to produce.

Correct Answer Explanation:

If reusable cups require a significant amount of energy to produce, they may not be an eco-friendlier alternative.

Explanation for Incorrect Choices:

Choice A. Paper cups can be recycled. This is incorrect. Even though paper cups can be recycled, their production still contributes to deforestation.

Choice C. Deforestation is a leading cause of global warming. This is incorrect. This strengthens Jane's argument, as it provides another reason to reduce deforestation.

Choice D. Many coffee shops offer discounts to customers who bring their reusable cups. This is incorrect. This also strengthens Jane's argument by providing an incentive to use reusable cups.

Choice E. Using reusable cups can reduce waste in landfills. This is incorrect. This strengthens Jane's argument by presenting another benefit of using reusable cups.

***

Stimulus #21:

Correct Answer:

Choice A. The argument incorrectly equates correlation with causation.

Correct Answer Explanation:

Just because people who consume energy drinks report feeling more alert, it doesn't necessarily mean that the drinks are the cause of the increased alertness.

Explanation for Incorrect Choices:

Choice B. The argument is based on a biased sample. This is incorrect. The sample is not necessarily biased; it's simply those who frequently consume energy drinks.

Choice C. The argument fails to consider the potential negative effects of energy drinks. This is incorrect. The argument's scope is about the effectiveness of energy drinks in increasing alertness, not their potential negative effects.

Choice D. The argument relies on an appeal to popularity. This is incorrect. The argument is not suggesting that energy drinks are effective because they are popular.

Choice E. The argument does not provide a clear definition of what constitutes "alertness." This is incorrect. The argument may be imprecise, but this is not the primary flaw.

***

Stimulus #22:

Correct Answer:

Choice B. Public safety should be a priority, even if it requires limiting certain individual freedoms.

Correct Answer Explanation:

The city council is prioritizing public safety (minimizing pedestrian accidents) by limiting a freedom (using cell phones while crossing streets).

Explanation for Incorrect Choices:

Choice A. Laws should be created to regulate every aspect of people's lives. This is incorrect. This principle is overly broad and doesn't directly connect to the situation at hand.

Choice C. The freedom to use a cell phone whenever and wherever one wishes is a fundamental right. This is incorrect. This principle contradicts the council's decision.

Choice D. Pedestrian accidents are the leading cause of death in urban areas. This is incorrect. This principle does not justify the restriction on cellphone use, even though it emphasizes the severity of pedestrian accidents.

Choice E. Cell phones are unnecessary distractions and should be eliminated. This is incorrect. This principle is extreme and does not align with the council's specific decision about cellphone use while crossing streets.

* * *

Stimulus #23:

Correct Answer:

Choice C. The new policies will be successful in reducing greenhouse gas emissions.

Correct Answer Explanation:

The stimulus clearly states that if the policies are enforced and adhered to, the emission levels will be reduced.

Explanation for Incorrect Choices:

Choice A. The government's policies from last year were not targeting major industrial contributors. This is incorrect. The stimulus does not provide information about the specifics of last year's policies.

Choice B. Major industrial contributors are the primary source of greenhouse gas emissions. This is incorrect. While it is implied that industrial contributors play a significant role, it doesn't necessarily mean they are the primary source.

Choice D. The new policies are better than the policies from the previous year. This is incorrect. The passage doesn't allow us to compare the quality of this year's policies to last year's.

Choice E. The government failed to enforce the policies last year. This is incorrect. The reason for last year's failure is not discussed in the passage.

*　*　*

Stimulus #24:

Correct Answer:

Choice D. Just as a mechanic needs to remove faulty parts from a car for it to run well, a doctor must remove unhealthy tissues for a patient to recover.

Correct Answer Explanation:

Like the original statement, this involves removing something negative (faulty car parts, unhealthy tissues) for something positive (car running well, patient's recovery).

Explanation for Incorrect Choices:

Choice A. To make a delicious soup, the chef must use fresh ingredients, just as a painter needs quality paints to create a good painting. This is incorrect. This comparison does not involve removing a negative element for a positive outcome.

Choice B. Like a conductor leading an orchestra to create harmonious music, a project manager must coordinate a team to accomplish a project successfully. This is incorrect. This does not follow the pattern of needing to eliminate something for another thing to thrive.

Choice C. An athlete needs to follow a rigorous training routine to excel, just as a pilot needs rigorous training to fly a plane. This is incorrect. The training routines in both instances are positive elements, not distractions or barriers that need to be removed.

Choice E. A well-trained dog obeys its master's commands just like a well-programmed computer executes commands. This is incorrect. This involves obedience and execution, not the removal of a negative factor for a positive outcome.

***

Stimulus #25:

Correct Answer:

Choice A. The students who played sports also reported having better time management skills than those who did not play sports.

Correct Answer Explanation:

This introduces an alternative cause for the higher GPA — time management skills — weakening the argument that playing sports is the primary reason for the higher GPA.

Explanation for Incorrect Choices:

Choice B. The survey was conducted only in one university, not nationwide. This is incorrect. Although the scope of the survey could impact the generalizability of its findings, it does not weaken the causal claim made in the argument.

Choice C. There are some students who do not play sports but still have high GPAs. This is incorrect. While this answer choice indicates that sports isn't the only path to high GPA, it doesn't undermine the claim that sports can improve academic performance.

Choice D. The students who played sports also reported getting more sleep on average than those who did not play sports. This is incorrect. Similar to answer choice A, this introduces another possible cause for higher GPA. However, it does not directly weaken the claim that sports improve academic performance as much as A does.

Choice E. The majority of the students surveyed did not play sports. This is incorrect. The participation rate does not impact the causal relationship in the argument.

***

III

Analytical Reasoning
(Logic Games)

11

Introduction to Analytical Reasoning

The Analytical Reasoning section of the LSAT presents test takers with a series of Logic Games, which require logical analysis and strategic thinking to solve. This section evaluates your ability to understand and manipulate complex relationships between elements and your aptitude for making deductions and inferences based on given rules and conditions. Mastering the Analytical Reasoning section is crucial for achieving a high score on the LSAT.

The Challenge:

Analytical Reasoning challenges test takers in several ways: Firstly, it demands strong organizational and diagramming skills to visually represent the relationships and constraints provided in each Logic Game. Effectively organizing the information allows for a clearer understanding of the rules and enables you to make accurate deductions. Furthermore, the section requires you to efficiently manage your time, as each Logic Game typically consists of multiple questions to be answered within a specified time limit.

Another significant challenge in Analytical Reasoning is the need to think both analytically and creatively. While the rules and conditions of the Logic Games provide a framework, successfully navigating through the games often requires thinking outside the box and exploring various possibilities and hypothetical scenarios. This ability to think flexibly and adaptively is essential for effectively solving the complex puzzles presented in this section.

The Approach:

It is important to approach the Analytical Reasoning section with a systematic and methodical strategy. This includes understanding the different types of Logic Games commonly encountered, such as sequencing, grouping, and matching games, and familiarizing yourself with the specific rules and patterns associated with each game type. Additionally, practicing sample Logic Games and honing your analytical skills will contribute to your success in this section.

How LSAT Prep Guide Helps:

In this LSAT Prep Guide, we will provide you with comprehensive strategies, techniques, and practice exercises to conquer the challenges posed by the Analytical Reasoning section. By developing your logical reasoning abilities, refining your diagramming techniques, and mastering the art of efficient time management, you will be well-equipped to approach each Logic Game with confidence and precision.

12

Techniques for Diagramming and Solving Different Types of Logic Games

In the Analytical Reasoning section of the LSAT, mastering the techniques for diagramming and solving different types of Logic Games is essential. Each Logic Game presents a unique set of rules and conditions, requiring test takers to employ specific strategies to analyze and solve the puzzles effectively. This section provides an overview of the techniques that can be employed for diagramming and solving different types of Logic Games.

Ordering Games:

- **Establish a clear ordering system:** Use a visual representation, such as a number line or a grid, to depict the sequential relationships between elements.
- **Deduce and infer information:** Analyze the given rules and make deductions to determine the possible positions and order of elements.
- **Utilize notations and symbols:** Employ symbols, abbreviations, or shorthand to represent the constraints and relationships between elements.
- **Track and eliminate possibilities:** Keep track of the valid and invalid scenarios as you make deductions, using elimination strategies to narrow down the possibilities.

Grouping Games:

- **Create accurate and organized diagrams:** Use visual diagrams, such as tables or diagrams with circles or squares, to represent the groups and their relationships.
- **Identify restrictions and inferences:** Analyze the given rules to identify any fixed relationships, limitations, or restrictions that govern the grouping.
- **Make hypothetical scenarios:** Consider different scenarios based on the given rules to explore potential solutions and eliminate incorrect options.
- **Utilize notations and symbols:** Employ symbols or notations to represent group membership or exclusions, and track the interrelationships between elements.

Matching Games:

- Create a clear representation of the matching relationships: Use visual diagrams, tables, or grids to illustrate the matching relationships between elements.
- Identify constraints and possibilities: Analyze the given rules to determine any fixed or variable relationships between the elements being matched.

- **Utilize notations and symbols:** Employ symbols or notations to represent the matching relationships and track the available options.
- **Utilize elimination strategies**: Eliminate incorrect options based on the given rules and deductions made during the game.

Practicing these techniques extensively and developing familiarity with different types of Logic Games is crucial. Doing so will enhance your ability to effectively diagram and solve Logic Games within the time constraints of the LSAT. Regular practice and exposure to a wide range of Logic Games will sharpen your analytical thinking, pattern recognition, and deduction-making skills.

This LSAT Prep Guide provides detailed explanations and examples of each type of Logic Game, along with step-by-step guidance on applying the diagramming and solving techniques outlined above. By mastering these techniques, you will be well-prepared to approach any Logic Game with confidence and precision, ultimately improving your performance in the Analytical Reasoning section of the LSAT.

13

Strategies for Time Management and Maximizing Efficiency

In the Analytical Reasoning section of the LSAT, effective time management and maximizing efficiency are crucial for successfully navigating the Logic Games and maximizing your overall score. This section outlines strategies to help you optimize your time and improve efficiency when solving Logic Games.

Set a Time Allocation Plan:

- **Allocate a specific amount of time to each Logic Game:** Read the instructions and assess the complexity of the game to determine how much time to allocate for each game.
- **Prioritize games based on difficulty:** Identify the easier and more manageable games to solve first, as this will allow you to gain momentum and build confidence.
- **Stick to your allocated time:** Be mindful of the time allocated for each game and avoid spending excessive time on a single game, even if you encounter difficulties.

Develop an Effective Game Approach:

- **Carefully read and analyze the rules:** Take the time to thoroughly understand the given rules and conditions before starting to solve the questions.
- **Identify inferences and make deductions:** Look for logical deductions that can be made based on the given rules, which will help you make efficient progress in solving the game.
- **Utilize efficient diagramming techniques:** Use clear and concise diagramming methods that suit the specific game type to effectively represent the relationships and constraints.
- **Focus on the main objective:** Stay focused on the ultimate goal of answering the questions accurately rather than getting caught up in unnecessary details.

Practice with Time Constraints:

- **Use timed practice sessions:** Incorporate timed practice sessions into your study routine to simulate the time pressure experienced during the actual LSAT.
- **Develop a pacing strategy:** Experiment with different pacing techniques, such as allocating specific time limits to each question or section, to find the approach that works best for you.
- **Increase familiarity with question types:** Through regular practice, become familiar with the common question types and develop strategies for approaching each type efficiently.

Avoid Common Time-Wasting Traps:

- **Don't get stuck on difficult questions:** If you encounter a challenging question, make an educated guess and move on to maximize your overall score potential.
- **Be cautious with time-consuming deductions:** While deductions are important, avoid spending excessive time making elaborate deductions that may not be necessary for solving the game efficiently.
- **Limit erasing and redrawing:** Minimize unnecessary erasing and redrawing to save time and maintain clarity in your diagrams.

By implementing these strategies for time management and efficiency, you will enhance your ability to tackle the Logic Games effectively within the given time constraints of the LSAT. Regular practice and exposure to a variety of Logic Games will help you develop a sense of timing and improve your decision-making skills under pressure.

In this LSAT Prep Guide, we provide guidance on time management strategies, along with ample opportunities to practice timed Logic Games. By applying these strategies and refining your approach, you will be well-prepared to approach the Analytical Reasoning section confidently, efficiently, and precisely, ultimately improving your overall LSAT performance.

14

Practice Exercise 1

Logic Game 1

There are six friends — Mia, Nia, Lia, Tia, Via, and Ria — who are planning to watch six different movies in a local film festival over the course of six consecutive days, starting from Monday and ending on Saturday. The films they are watching are: "Under the Sun", "Moonlight Sonata", "Star Struck", "Clouded Judgment", "Rainbow's End", and "Wind Walker". Each friend watches exactly one film per day, according to the following conditions:

1. Lia watches a film before Mia and Nia.
2. Ria watches a film immediately after "Star Struck" is watched.
3. "Under the Sun" is watched before "Rainbow's End" but after "Clouded Judgment".
4. Via watches a film on Wednesday.
5. "Moonlight Sonata" is watched on the day immediately before Tia watches a film.

Question 1: Rule Check

If "Under the Sun" is watched on Wednesday, which of the following must be true?

A.) Ria watches a movie on Tuesday.
B.) Mia watches a movie on Friday.
C.) "Star Struck" is watched on Thursday.
D.) Via watches "Moonlight Sonata".
E.) "Wind Walker" is watched on Saturday.

Question 2: Rule Substitution

Which of the following, if substituted for the condition that Via watches a film on Wednesday, would have the same effect in determining the order of the film?

A.) Via does not watch a film on Monday or Tuesday.
B.) Via watches a film before Tia.
C.) Via watches a film after "Moonlight Sonata" is watched.
D.) Via does not watch "Star Struck".
E.) Via watches a film on a day immediately before or after "Moonlight Sonata" is watched.

Logic Game 2

Six friends — Frank, George, Harry, Ivan, Jack, and Karl — are deciding to split into two groups for a team event. Each group should have three friends. The groups are formed according to the following conditions:

1. If Frank is in a group, George must also be in the same group.
2. Harry and Ivan can't be in the same group.
3. Karl can only be in a group if Jack is not in the same group.
4. If Ivan is in a group with George, Jack must also be in the same group.

Question 1: Rule Check

Which of the following groups can be formed?

A.) Frank, George, Harry
B.) Ivan, Jack, Karl
C.) Frank, George, Ivan
D.) Harry, Ivan, Karl
E.) Frank, Ivan, Jack

Question 2: Must Be / Could Be

If Ivan and George are in the same group, which of the following must be true?

A.) Frank is in the same group as Ivan and George.
B.) Jack is in the same group as Ivan and George.
C.) Harry is in the opposite group of Ivan, George, and Jack.
D.) Karl is in the same group as Harry.
E.) Karl is in the same group as Ivan and George.

***

Logic Game 3

A community garden has six plots — 1 through 6 — which will be filled with vegetables by six gardeners — Alice, Bob, Charlie, Dana, Eve, and Frank. Each gardener chooses one plot. The plots are assigned according to the following conditions:

1. Alice's plot must be to the immediate right of Bob's plot.
2. Dana can't have a plot next to Charlie's.
3. Frank's plot is somewhere to the left of Dana's plot.
4. Eve's plot is not at either end.

Question 1: Rule Check

Which of the following could be a possible arrangement of plots from 1 to 6?

A.) Bob, Alice, Charlie, Eve, Dana, Frank
B.) Charlie, Frank, Bob, Alice, Dana, Eve
C.) Bob, Alice, Frank, Dana, Charlie, Eve
D.) Frank, Charlie, Bob, Alice, Dana, Eve
E.) Alice, Bob, Charlie, Eve, Frank, Dana

Question 2: Minimum / Maximum

If Alice chooses plot number 3, which of the following must be true?

A.) Bob chooses plot number 2.
B.) Frank can't choose plot number 6.
C.) Charlie can't choose plot number 4.
D.) Dana chooses plot number 5.
E.) Eve chooses plot number 4.

***

Logic Game 4

In a small international conference, five delegates — Alice, Bob, Charlie, Dana, and Eve — each from a different country, are seated at a round table. The seating arrangement is to follow these conditions:

1. Alice can't sit next to Charlie or Dana.
2. Bob has to sit next to Dana.
3. Eve can't sit next to Bob.
4. Charlie sits somewhere to the right of Eve.

Question 1: Rule Check

Which of the following could be a possible seating arrangement, in clockwise order starting from Alice?

A.) Alice, Bob, Dana, Eve, Charlie
B.) Alice, Eve, Charlie, Bob, Dana
C.) Alice, Bob, Charlie, Eve, Dana
D.) Alice, Dana, Bob, Eve, Charlie
E.) Alice, Charlie, Bob, Dana, Eve

Question 2: Rule Substitution

If Rule 4 (Charlie sits somewhere to the right of Eve) is replaced by "Charlie sits next to Eve," which of the following must be true?

A.) Charlie sits next to Alice.
B.) Bob sits next to Alice.
C.) Dana sits next to Charlie.
D.) Eve does not sit next to Bob.
E.) Dana does not sit next to Eve.

***

15

Practice Exercise 2

Logic Game 1

A local charity is organizing a charity run. Six runners - Tom, Jane, Harry, Sarah, Nick, and Mary - are participating in the race. They will finish the race in a sequential order from first to sixth. The following conditions must hold:

1. Harry finishes before Sarah but after Tom.
2. Mary does not finish immediately before or immediately after Nick.
3. Jane finishes somewhere after Harry.

Question 1: Rule Check

If Tom finishes third, which one of the following could be a possible order of finish for the runners?

A.) Nick, Mary, Tom, Harry, Sarah, Jane
B.) Mary, Nick, Tom, Jane, Harry, Sarah
C.) Sarah, Mary, Tom, Nick, Harry, Jane
D.) Nick, Tom, Mary, Harry, Sarah, Jane
E.) Jane, Mary, Tom, Harry, Sarah, Nick

Question 2: Must Be / Could Be

If Sarah finishes fourth, which one of the following must be true?

A.) Tom finishes first.
B.) Harry finishes third.
C.) Nick finishes fifth.
D.) Jane finishes last.
E.) Mary finishes second.

***

Logic Game 2

Consider a street where five friends — Alex, Ben, Chris, Dave, and Eric — live. The houses are arranged linearly, and each friend lives in a different house. They've agreed to these conditions:

1. Alex lives somewhere to the left of Ben.
2. Chris lives between Ben and Dave.
3. Eric does not live in any of the two houses at the ends.
4. Ben's house is not next to Eric's house.

Question 1: Rule Check

Which of the following could be the order of houses from left to right?

A.) Alex, Ben, Chris, Dave, Eric
B.) Chris, Alex, Ben, Eric, Dave
C.) Ben, Chris, Eric, Alex, Dave
D.) Dave, Chris, Ben, Alex, Eric
E.) Alex, Eric, Ben, Chris, Dave

Question 2: Rule Substitution

Which of the following rules, if substituted for the rule that Ben's house is not next to Eric's house, would have the same effect on the arrangement of the houses?

A.) Ben's house is to the right of Eric's house.
B.) Eric's house is somewhere to the left of Ben's house.
C.) Ben's house is somewhere to the left of Eric's house.
D.) Eric's house is not next to Alex's house.
E.) Alex's house is not next to Ben's house.

* * *

Logic Game 3

Four friends - Olivia, Patrick, Quinn, and Rachel - are playing a unique board game. The game has four different types of characters - Archer, Barbarian, Cleric, and Druid. Each friend plays as a different character.

The rules of their choices are:

1. Olivia does not play as the Cleric or the Druid.
2. Patrick plays a character that is alphabetically before Olivia's character.
3. Quinn plays a character that is alphabetically after Rachel's character.
4. Rachel does not play as the Archer.

Question 1: Rule Check

If Quinn plays as the Druid, which one of the following must be true?

A.) Olivia plays as the Barbarian.
B.) Patrick plays as the Archer.
C.) Rachel plays as the Cleric.
D.) Patrick plays as the Barbarian.
E.) Rachel plays as the Barbarian.

Question 2: New Information / Conditions

Suppose Olivia ends up playing as the Barbarian. Which of the following could be a possible arrangement of characters?

A.) Olivia - Barbarian, Patrick - Archer, Quinn - Druid, Rachel - Cleric.
B.) Olivia - Barbarian, Patrick - Archer, Quinn - Cleric, Rachel - Druid.
C.) Olivia - Barbarian, Patrick - Druid, Quinn - Cleric, Rachel - Archer.
D.) Olivia - Barbarian, Patrick - Cleric, Quinn - Druid, Rachel - Archer.
E.) Olivia - Barbarian, Patrick - Archer, Quinn - Archer, Rachel - Druid.

***

Logic Game 4

The annual town carnival is taking place this weekend. Four performers - Mark, Nola, Ophelia, and Paul - are scheduled to perform magic, juggling, stand-up comedy, and mime act, but not necessarily in that order. The performances will happen one after the other without any breaks.

The scheduling rules are as follows:

1. Mark performs before Nola, but after the magic act.
2. The stand-up comedy act takes place after the mime act, but before the juggling.
3. Ophelia performs either immediately before or immediately after Paul.

Question 1: Rule Check

Given the rules above, which one of the following could be a possible order of performers?

A.) Mark (Magic), Nola (Juggling), Ophelia (Mime), Paul (Stand-up Comedy)
B.) Ophelia (Magic), Paul (Mime), Mark (Stand-up Comedy), Nola (Juggling)
C.) Paul (Magic), Mark (Mime), Nola (Stand-up Comedy), Ophelia (Juggling)
D.) Paul (Mime), Ophelia (Stand-up Comedy), Mark (Magic), Nola (Juggling)
E.) Mark (Mime), Paul (Magic), Ophelia (Stand-up Comedy), Nola (Juggling)

Question 2: New Information / Conditions

Suppose the mime act is performed by Paul. Which one of the following could be true?

A.) Ophelia performs the magic act.
B.) Mark performs the stand-up comedy act.
C.) Nola performs the juggling act.
D.) Mark performs the juggling act.
E.) Nola performs the mime act.

***

16

Practice Exercise 1: Answers and Explanations

Logic Game 1

Question 1: Answer and Reasoning

Answer: E. "Wind Walker" is watched on Saturday.

1. If "Under the Sun" is watched on Wednesday, according to rule 3, "Clouded Judgment" must be watched before it, so "Clouded Judgment" is watched on Monday or Tuesday.
2. Also, "Rainbow's End" must be watched after "Under the Sun", so it must be on Thursday, Friday, or Saturday.
3. Via cannot watch "Under the Sun" because she is watching a movie on Wednesday, and Lia must watch before Mia and Nia, so Lia cannot watch on Wednesday either.
4. Since "Moonlight Sonata" must be watched on the day immediately before Tia watches a film, "Moonlight Sonata" cannot be watched on Saturday, so Tia cannot watch a movie on Sunday. The only remaining movie is "Wind Walker", so "Wind Walker" is watched on Saturday.

Question 1: Wrong Answer Explanations

A.) Incorrect. There's no rule that Ria must watch a movie on Tuesday. Ria watches a movie immediately after "Star Struck" is watched, but there's no information on when "Star Struck" is watched.
B.) Incorrect. Mia can watch a movie on any day after Lia watches her movie. There's no rule stating that Mia must watch a movie on Friday.
C.) Incorrect. We have no information stating that "Star Struck" must be watched on Thursday.
D.) Incorrect. Via can watch any movie on Wednesday. There's no rule stating that Via must watch "Moonlight Sonata".

Question 2: Answer and Reasoning

Answer: A. Via does not watch a film on Monday or Tuesday.

Replacing the rule "Via watches a film on Wednesday" with "Via does not watch a film on Monday or Tuesday would still satisfy all the other constraints:

104

1. Lia watches a film before Mia and Nia.
2. Ria watches a film immediately after "Star Struck" is watched.
3. "Under the Sun" is watched before "Rainbow's End" but after "Clouded Judgment".
4. "Moonlight Sonata" is watched on the day immediately before Tia watches a film.

Under this new rule, Via still has only one option which is to watch the film on Wednesday, so the change would have the same effect as the original rule.

Question 2: Wrong Answer Explanations

B.) Incorrect. Via watching a film before Tia does not necessarily mean she watches a film on Wednesday. It could also be on Monday, Tuesday, or Thursday.

C.) Incorrect. Via watching a film after "Moonlight Sonata" is watched does not mean she watches a film on Wednesday. "Moonlight Sonata" could be watched on any day from Monday to Friday, meaning Via could watch her film on any day from Tuesday to Saturday.

D.) Incorrect. Via not watching "Star Struck" does not restrict her to watching a film on Wednesday. She still has five other films to watch and can watch them on any day.

E.) Incorrect. Via watching a film on a day immediately before or after "Moonlight Sonata" is watched does not mean she watches a film on Wednesday. Via could watch a film on Tuesday if "Moonlight Sonata" is watched on Monday, or on Thursday if "Moonlight Sonata" is watched on Wednesday, or on Friday if "Moonlight Sonata" is watched on Thursday.

***

Logic Game 2

Question 1: Answer and Reasoning

Answer: A. Frank, George, Harry

This group abides by all conditions:

1. Frank and George are together (Condition 1).
2. Harry is in the group, and Ivan isn't (Condition 2).
3. Karl is not in the group, so the presence or absence of Jack doesn't matter (Condition 3).
4. Ivan isn't in the group, so the presence or absence of Jack and George doesn't matter (Condition 4).

Question 1: Wrong Answer Explanations

B.) Incorrect. Ivan and Karl can't be in the same group (Condition 3).
C.) Incorrect. Ivan, George, and Frank can be together, but Jack must also be there (Condition 4).
D.) Incorrect. Harry and Ivan can't be in the same group (Condition 2).
E.) Incorrect. If Ivan is in the group, and Frank is there, then George must also be there (Conditions 1 and 4).

Question 2: Answer and Reasoning

Answer: B. Jack is in the same group as Ivan and George.

If Ivan and George are in the same group, according to condition 4, Jack must also be in the same group.

Question 2: Wrong Answer Explanations

A.) Incorrect. Although Frank usually is with George, the condition allowing Ivan to be with George requires Jack to be present, not Frank.
C.) Incorrect. Harry being in the opposite group of Ivan, George, and Jack is possible but not a necessity.
D.) Incorrect. Karl being in the same group as Harry is possible but not a necessity.
E.) Incorrect. Karl and Ivan can't be in the same group (Condition 3).

***

Logic Game 3

Question 1: Answer and Reasoning

Answer: D. Frank, Charlie, Bob, Alice, Dana, Eve

This arrangement abides by all conditions:

1. Alice's plot (4) is to the immediate right of Bob's (3).
2. Dana's plot (5) isn't next to Charlie's (2).
3. Frank's plot (1) is to the left of Dana's (5).
4. Eve's plot (6) isn't at either end.

Question 1: Wrong Answer Explanations

A.) Incorrect. Frank's plot should be to the left of Dana's.
B.) Incorrect. Dana's plot is next to Charlie's which contradicts the second condition.
C.) Incorrect. Eve's plot is at the end which contradicts the fourth condition.
E.) Incorrect. Alice's plot should be to the immediate right of Bob's.

Question 2: Answer and Reasoning

Answer: A. Bob chooses plot number 2.

If Alice chooses plot number 3, according to the first condition, Bob must choose plot number 2.

Question 2: Wrong Answer Explanations

B.) Incorrect. The conditions do not prevent Frank from choosing plot number 6.
C.) Incorrect. The conditions do not prevent Charlie from choosing plot number 4.
D.) Incorrect. The conditions do not require Dana to choose plot number 5.
E.) Incorrect. The conditions do not require Eve to choose plot number 4.

***

Logic Game 4

Question 1: Answer and Reasoning

Answer: B. Alice, Eve, Charlie, Bob, Dana

This arrangement meets all conditions:

1. Alice is not sitting next to Charlie or Dana.
2. Bob is sitting next to Dana.
3. Eve is not sitting next to Bob.
4. Charlie is sitting to the right of Eve.

Question 1: Wrong Answer Explanations

A.) Incorrect. Alice can't sit next to Dana.
C.) Incorrect. Alice can't sit next to Charlie, and Eve can't sit next to Bob.
D.) Incorrect. Bob isn't sitting next to Dana.
E.) Incorrect. Alice can't sit next to Charlie, and Eve isn't to the right of Charlie.

Question 2: Answer and Reasoning

Answer: D. Eve does not sit next to Bob.

If Charlie sits next to Eve, the condition that Eve can't sit next to Bob (condition 3) must still hold. Hence, Eve does not sit next to Bob.

Question 2: Wrong Answer Explanations

A.) Incorrect. There's no condition that requires Charlie to sit next to Alice.
B.) Incorrect. There's no condition that requires Bob to sit next to Alice.
C.) Incorrect. There's no condition that requires Dana to sit next to Charlie.
E.) Incorrect. With the new rule, Dana could potentially sit next to Eve.

***

17

Practice Exercise 2: Answers and Explanations

Logic Game 1

Question 1: Answer and Reasoning

Answer: A. Nick, Mary, Tom, Harry, Sarah, Jane

This arrangement meets all conditions:

1. Harry (4th) finishes before Sarah (5th) but after Tom (3rd).
2. Mary (2nd) does not finish immediately before or immediately after Nick (1st).
3. Jane (6th) finishes somewhere after Harry (4th).

Question 1: Wrong Answer Explanations

B.) Incorrect. Jane (4th) cannot finish before Harry (5th).
C.) Incorrect. Sarah (1st) cannot finish before Tom (3rd) and Harry (5th).
D.) Incorrect. Mary (3rd) cannot finish immediately after Nick (4th).
E.) Incorrect. Jane (1st) cannot finish before Tom (3rd) and Harry (4th).

Question 2: Answer and Reasoning

Answer: B. Harry finishes third.

If Sarah finishes fourth, then Harry must finish before her. Since Harry also finishes after Tom, Harry must finish third.

Question 2: Wrong Answer Explanations

A.) Incorrect. Tom could finish in positions 1 or 2.
C.) Incorrect. Nick could finish in any position except 4th and 5th.
D.) Incorrect. Jane could finish in positions 5 or 6.
E.) Incorrect. Mary could finish in any position except 4th and 5th.

***

Logic Game 2

Question 1: Answer and Reasoning

Answer: A. Alex, Ben, Chris, Dave, Eric

This order satisfies all the conditions:

1. Alex is to the left of Ben (Condition 1).
2. Chris is between Ben and Dave (Condition 2).
3. Eric is not at the ends (Condition 3).
4. Ben's house is not next to Eric's house (Condition 4).

Question 1: Wrong Answer Explanations

B.) Incorrect. Alex is not to the left of Ben (Condition 1).
C.) Incorrect. Chris is not between Ben and Dave (Condition 2).
D.) Incorrect. Alex is not to the left of Ben (Condition 1).
E.) Incorrect. Chris is not between Ben and Dave (Condition 2).

Question 2: Answer and Reasoning

Answer: B. Eric's house is somewhere to the left of Ben's house.

If Eric's house is to the left of Ben's house, it implicitly implies that Ben's house can't be next to Eric's house because Alex's house is already there. So, this rule would have the same effect as the rule that Ben's house is not next to Eric's house.

Question 2: Wrong Answer Explanations

A.) Incorrect. This rule would allow Ben's house to be next to Eric's house.
C.) Incorrect. This rule would place Eric's house next to Ben's, violating the original rule.
D.) Incorrect. This rule doesn't guarantee that Ben's house won't be next to Eric's house.
E.) Incorrect. This rule doesn't affect the location of Eric's house relative to Ben's house.

***

Logic Game 3

Question 1: Answer and Reasoning

Answer: C. Rachel plays as the Cleric.

If Quinn plays as the Druid (Rule 3), Rachel must play as the Cleric because it's the only choice alphabetically before Druid and isn't played by Olivia (Rule 1).

Question 1: Wrong Answer Explanations

A.) Incorrect. Olivia could play either the Archer or the Barbarian.
B.) Incorrect. Patrick could play either the Archer or the Barbarian.
D.) Incorrect. Patrick cannot play as the Barbarian as it would contradict Rule 2, since it comes after Archer in alphabetical order, the only other option for Olivia.
E.) Incorrect. Rachel cannot play as the Barbarian since she must play a character that comes alphabetically before Quinn's character (Rule 3).

Question 2: Answer and Reasoning

Answer: A. Olivia - Barbarian, Patrick - Archer, Quinn - Druid, Rachel - Cleric.

If Olivia is the Barbarian, then Patrick must be the Archer (Rule 2). Rachel must be the Cleric since it's the only character left for her that is alphabetically before Quinn's character. Quinn is then left with the Druid.

Question 2: Wrong Answer Explanations

B.) Incorrect. Rachel cannot play the Druid because that would violate Rule 3 (Quinn must play a character that comes alphabetically after Rachel's).
C.) Incorrect. Patrick cannot play the Druid, as Patrick plays a character that is alphabetically before Olivia's character (Rule 2).
D.) Incorrect. Quinn cannot play the Druid in this scenario because it would violate Rule 3 (Quinn's character must come alphabetically after Rachel's).
E.) Incorrect. There are two Archers in this arrangement, which contradicts the initial condition that each friend plays a different character.

***

Logic Game 4

Question 1: Answer and Reasoning

Answer: B. Ophelia (Magic), Paul (Mime), Mark (Stand-up Comedy), Nola (Juggling)

Ophelia and Paul must be adjacent according to Rule 3. The only way for them to both fit into the schedule and for all other conditions to be met is if Ophelia goes first with magic, followed by Paul with mime, then Mark doing stand-up, and finally, Nola doing juggling.

Question 1: Wrong Answer Explanations

A.) Incorrect. The stand-up comedy act cannot happen last because it needs to be before the juggling act according to Rule 2.

C.) Incorrect. Mark can't perform a mime act since it must be before his performance according to Rule 1.

D.) Incorrect. The stand-up comedy act cannot happen second because it needs to be before the juggling act according to Rule 2.

E.) Incorrect. The stand-up comedy act cannot happen third because it needs to be before the juggling act according to Rule 2.

Question 2: Answer and Reasoning

Answer: C. Nola performs the juggling act.

Given Paul is performing the mime act, and it is mentioned that the stand-up comedy act takes place after the mime act (Rule 2), and since Mark is before Nola (Rule 1), the only place for Nola in the sequence would be at the end. Thus, she performs the juggling act which is the last performance.If Charlie sits next to Eve, the condition that Eve can't sit next to Bob (condition 3) must still hold. Hence, Eve does not sit next to Bob.

Question 2: Wrong Answer Explanations

A.) Incorrect. Ophelia cannot perform the magic act because Mark performs after the magic act and before Nola according to Rule 1. In this case, Ophelia has to perform after Paul, not before.

B.) Incorrect. Mark cannot perform the stand-up comedy act as it is before the juggling and after the mime, Mark has to be before Nola (Rule 1) who in this case performs the juggling act.

D.) Incorrect. Mark cannot perform the juggling act as Mark must perform before Nola according to Rule 1. In this scenario, Nola performs the juggling act.

E.) Incorrect. Nola cannot perform the mime act because Paul is assigned to perform the mime act according to the new condition.

***

IV
Reading Comprehension

18

Introduction to Reading Comprehension

The Reading Comprehension section of the LSAT evaluates a test taker's ability to understand complex passages and draw accurate and insightful conclusions from them. This section assesses critical reading skills, including the capacity to analyze and interpret written material effectively. A strong performance in the Reading Comprehension section is essential for achieving a high score on the LSAT.

The primary objective of the Reading Comprehension section is to assess your ability to comprehend and synthesize information from a variety of written sources. This section presents passages from diverse subject areas, such as humanities, social sciences, natural sciences, and law-related topics. The passages are typically written in a dense and sophisticated manner, challenging you to grasp the author's main ideas, evaluate arguments, and identify implicit assumptions.

The Reading Comprehension section aims to evaluate the following skills:

Comprehension and Analysis:

- Understand the main ideas, themes, and purpose of the passage.
- Identify the author's tone, attitude, and perspective.
- Grasp the relationships between ideas and the logical structure of the passage.
- Recognize the organization and development of the passage's content.

Reasoning and Evaluation:

- Evaluate the strength of arguments presented in the passage.
- Assess the validity of claims and supporting evidence.
- Identify assumptions and implications made by the author.
- Distinguish between fact and opinion.

Synthesis and Inference:

- Draw accurate and reasonable inferences based on the information presented.
- Synthesize information from different parts of the passage to form a comprehensive understanding.
- Make connections between the passage and external knowledge or experiences.
- Identify the implications and consequences of the ideas presented.

To excel in the Reading Comprehension section, it is crucial to develop effective reading strategies and employ active reading techniques. These include previewing the passage, identifying the passage's structure, actively engaging with the content, taking concise notes, and summarizing the main points. Additionally, improving your vocabulary, honing your ability to analyze arguments, and practicing reading complex texts will contribute to your success in this section.

In this LSAT Prep Guide, we provide comprehensive guidance and strategies to help you enhance your reading comprehension skills. By practicing with various passage types, learning effective reading techniques, and familiarizing yourself with the question types encountered in this section, you will develop the necessary tools to approach the Reading Comprehension section with confidence and achieve optimal results on the LSAT.

19

Active Reading Strategies

The Reading Comprehension section of the LSAT presents test takers with complex passages that require careful analysis and comprehension. To navigate through these passages successfully, active reading strategies play a crucial role in enhancing understanding and maximizing performance. This section outlines effective strategies for actively engaging with and comprehending complex passages.

Preview the Passage:

- Begin by quickly skimming the passage to get an overall sense of its structure, main ideas, and topic.
- Pay attention to headings, subheadings, and topic sentences to grasp the organization and flow of the passage.
- Note any bolded or italicized text, as they often highlight important information or key terms.

Identify the Passage Structure:

- Determine the passage's main purpose, whether it aims to present an argument, provide information, or analyze a topic.
- Identify the introductory section, body paragraphs, and conclusion to understand the logical progression of ideas.
- Look for transition words and phrases that connect ideas or signal shifts in the author's reasoning.

Engage Actively with the Content:

- Read the passage actively, focusing on comprehension and retaining key information.
- Highlight or underline important points, main ideas, and supporting evidence as you read.
- Take concise notes or make marginal annotations to summarize key arguments or capture your own thoughts and reactions.

Identify Key Elements:

- Recognize the main ideas and arguments presented by the author.
- Pay attention to supporting evidence, examples, or data that validate the author's claims or illustrate concepts.

- Identify any counterarguments or contrasting viewpoints the author presents.

Summarize and Paraphrase:

- Periodically pause and summarize the passage in your own words, ensuring you have a clear understanding of the content.
- Paraphrase key points or arguments to reinforce comprehension and aid in recall.
- Practice condensing complex ideas into concise summaries without losing their essential meaning.

Make Connections and Inferences:

- Relate the information in the passage to your prior knowledge and experiences.
- Draw inferences and make logical connections between different parts of the passage.
- Consider the implications and consequences of the ideas presented by the author.

By employing these active reading strategies, you can enhance your comprehension of complex passages and effectively approach the Reading Comprehension section of the LSAT. Regular practice with diverse passage topics and exposure to a range of writing styles will further reinforce these skills.

In this LSAT Prep Guide, we provide guidance on implementing these active reading strategies through sample passages and practice exercises. By honing your ability to preview, analyze, summarize, and make connections within complex passages, you will sharpen your reading comprehension skills, ultimately leading to improved performance on the LSAT.

20
Reading Comprehension Strategic Approaches

In the Reading Comprehension section of the LSAT, effectively identifying the main ideas, understanding the passage's structure, and discerning the author's perspective is critical for comprehending complex passages. This section outlines approaches that can aid in the identification of main ideas, understanding passage structures, and analyzing the author's perspective.

Identify the Main Ideas:

- Look for topic sentences or thesis statements that express the central focus of the passage.
- Pay attention to repeated concepts, ideas, or arguments throughout the passage.
- Determine the main ideas by considering what the author emphasizes or spends the most time discussing.

Recognize Passage Structures:

- Identify the organization and structure of the passage, such as whether it follows a cause-effect, compare-contrast, or problem-solution pattern.
- Look for transitions, signposts, or keywords that indicate shifts between different sections or ideas.
- Pay attention to headings, subheadings, or other formatting elements that provide clues about the passage structure.

Analyze the Author's Perspective:

- Consider the author's tone, attitude, or bias toward the subject matter.
- Evaluate the author's purpose or intention in writing the passage, whether it is to inform, persuade, critique, or analyze.
- Examine the author's use of language, rhetoric, or persuasive techniques to understand their stance or viewpoint.

Look for Supporting Evidence and Examples:

- Identify the evidence, examples, or data presented by the author to support their arguments or claims.
- Evaluate the quality and relevance of the supporting evidence and how it contributes to the main ideas.

• Consider the credibility and reliability of the sources or references cited by the author.

<u>Consider the Author's Assumptions and Implications:</u>

• Identify any assumptions or underlying beliefs the author makes throughout the passage.
• Look for implications or consequences of the ideas presented by the author.
• Consider any potential limitations, biases, or gaps in the author's argument or perspective.

By employing these approaches, you can enhance your ability to identify main ideas, understand passage structures, and analyze the author's perspective effectively. Regular practice with a wide range of passages and exposure to various writing styles will further reinforce these skills.

In this LSAT Prep Guide, we provide guidance on implementing these approaches through sample passages and practice exercises. By practicing identifying main ideas, recognizing passage structures, and analyzing the author's perspective, you will develop a strong foundation in comprehending complex passages and improve your performance on the LSAT.

21

Reading Comprehension Exercise Details

The LSAT Reading Comprehension section typically contains four sets of reading questions, each set consisting of a passage and several questions related to that passage. The passages in this section are drawn from a variety of topics and sources, with one set of questions typically being about a pair of related passages.

Here's a broad overview of the structure:

1. **Passages:** Each passage is typically around 450-500 words. The topics generally fall into three categories: humanities, social sciences, and natural sciences. One of the four passages is usually a "Comparative Reading" passage, which includes two shorter, related passages.

2. **Questions:** Each passage is accompanied by 5-8 questions, for a total of approximately 26-28 questions in this section. The questions measure your ability to understand, analyze, and apply information you've read in the passages.

Here's a more detailed look at the question types you might encounter:

- **Main Idea Questions:** These ask about the central point or primary purpose of the passage.

- **Specific Detail Questions:** These ask about specific points or details mentioned in the passage.

- **Inference Questions:** These ask you to draw conclusions from information in the passage.

- **Function Questions:** These ask about why the author has chosen to include certain information or why certain phrases are used.

- **Tone/Attitude Questions:** These ask about the author's tone or attitude toward the information in the passage.

- **Structure/Organization Questions:** These ask about the overall structure of the passage, or how the author organizes information.

- **Analogy Questions:** These ask you to apply information or principles from the passage to a new situation.

- **Extrapolation Questions:** These ask you to consider how new information would affect the arguments or ideas in the passage.

- **Comparative Reading Questions:** These ask you to compare and contrast two related passages.

It's important to remember that the LSAT Reading Comprehension section is not simply about understanding the passage, but also about analyzing it and applying the information it contains. That requires both careful reading and logical reasoning.

22

Practice Exercise 1

Reading Passage #1

In 1963, Betty Friedan published "The Feminine Mystique," a landmark text in the history of the feminist movement. A response to the post-World War II phenomenon known as "the problem that has no name," which referred to the widespread dissatisfaction and restlessness felt by many American women, Friedan's book sparked a revolution. Friedan posited that women's dissatisfaction was a direct result of societal pressures to conform to traditional gender roles, which primarily relegated women to the home as wives and mothers.

The power of Friedan's work, however, lay not solely in its critique of society's prescribed gender roles but in its call for women to seek fulfillment outside of these roles. By urging women to pursue education and careers, Friedan suggested that women could find personal fulfillment and societal value in activities traditionally reserved for men. In doing so, she challenged the societal perception that women's worth was tied to their roles as homemakers.

Despite the significance of "The Feminine Mystique" and its impact on the feminist movement, critics argue that Friedan's work had significant limitations. The primary critique is that Friedan's perspective was largely centered on the experiences of white, middle-class women, thus neglecting the diverse experiences of women of color, working-class women, and other marginalized groups.

While these criticisms are valid, they do not diminish the impact of "The Feminine Mystique." Friedan's work prompted a critical examination of gender roles, inciting a shift in societal attitudes towards women's roles, and therefore served as a catalyst for the second-wave feminist movement.

Question #1

What is the main idea of the passage?

A.) The Feminine Mystique was a flawed book that overlooked the experiences of many women.
B.) Betty Friedan was a key figure in the second-wave feminist movement.
C.) The Feminine Mystique challenged traditional gender roles and sparked a societal shift in attitudes toward women's roles.
D.) The Feminine Mystique was solely a critique of society's prescribed gender roles.

Question #2

Which of the following statements is supported by the passage?

A.) Betty Friedan was critical of the feminist movement.
B.) The Feminine Mystique primarily addressed the needs of marginalized groups.
C.) The Feminine Mystique contributed to the onset of the second-wave feminist movement.
D.) Betty Friedan believed that a woman's worth was solely tied to her role as a homemaker.

Question #3

The author of the passage would most likely agree with which of the following statements about Betty Friedan?

A.) Friedan's emphasis on the plight of middle-class women undermined the broader goals of the feminist movement.
B.) Friedan's arguments in "The Feminine Mystique" were universally accepted by all women at the time of its publication.
C.) Friedan played a crucial role in raising awareness about the issues faced by women in the mid-20th century America.
D.) Friedan's writing was primarily inspired by her experiences as a marginalized woman.

Question #4

The primary purpose of the passage is to:

A.) Criticize Betty Friedan for her focus on middle-class women in "The Feminine Mystique".
B.) Analyze the impact of "The Feminine Mystique" on the feminist movement in the 1960s.
C.) Argue that "The Feminine Mystique" was the sole cause of the second-wave feminist movement.
D.) Offer a tribute to Betty Friedan for her contributions to the women's movement.

Question #5

Which of the following would the author most likely agree with?

A.) The Feminine Mystique was universally praised upon its release.
B.) Friedan's focus on middle-class women was a significant flaw in her work.
C.) The Feminine Mystique did more harm than good in advancing the cause of feminism.
D.) The Feminine Mystique played a crucial role in stimulating dialogue about women's societal roles.

Question #6

The author's primary purpose in the passage is to:

A) Critique the narrow focus of The Feminine Mystique on middle-class women.
B) Analyze the impact of The Feminine Mystique on the feminist movement.
C) Provide a detailed summary of The Feminine Mystique.
D) Argue that The Feminine Mystique was the most influential feminist work of the 20th century.

***

Reading Passage #2

Passage A

In the field of paleoanthropology, the discovery of the "Homo neanderthalensis" or the Neanderthal man significantly altered our understanding of human evolution. Initially, scientists believed that these beings were our ancestors; however, newer evidence suggests that they were a separate species altogether. Unlike the previously discovered Homo erectus, the Neanderthal man had a bigger brain cavity, a robust build, and unique cultural artifacts. This called into question the linear model of human evolution, suggesting a branching model instead.

Passage B

The recent findings in genomics suggest that the Neanderthals were not completely separate from Homo sapiens. In fact, present-day non-African humans have about 1-2% Neanderthal DNA. This suggests that interbreeding between the two species occurred when Homo sapiens migrated out of Africa. This evidence challenges the notion of a pure lineage of Homo sapiens, and underlines the complexity of human evolution.

Question #1

Which of the following best describes the relationship between the two passages?

A.) Passage B disputes a claim made in Passage A.
B.) Passage B extends an idea presented in Passage A.
C.) Passage B contradicts the conclusion drawn in Passage A.
D.) Passage A and Passage B discuss different aspects of the same topic.

Question #2

According to Passage B, what is the significance of the discovery that present-day non-African humans have about 1-2% Neanderthal DNA?

A.) It supports the notion that Neanderthals were a separate species.
B.) It validates the linear model of human evolution.
C.) It underscores the complexity of human evolution.
D.) It proves that Homo sapiens migrated out of Africa.

Question #3

How does Passage A's view on the human evolution model differ from Passage B's?

A.) Passage A believes in the multiregional model while Passage B supports the out-of-Africa model.
B.) Passage A advocates for the linear model while Passage B suggests a branching model.
C.) Passage A views Neanderthals as a distinct species, while Passage B views them as a sub-species of Homo sapiens.
D.) Passage A supports the out-of-Africa model while Passage B argues for a hybrid model of human evolution.

Question #4

Based on the passages, which of the following assertions about human evolution is true?

A.) Both passages explicitly support the out-of-Africa model of human evolution.
B.) Passage B disagrees with the idea of interbreeding among hominid species.
C.) Passage A suggests that the Neanderthals were completely replaced by Homo sapiens.
D.) Both passages argue that the multiregional model of human evolution is the most accurate.

Question #5

According to Passage A, which of the following would have been a likely argument made by supporters of the out-of-Africa model?

A.) Interbreeding between hominid species was an uncommon occurrence.
B.) Homo sapiens have genetic traces of other hominid species, such as Neanderthals.
C.) The genetic diversity among modern humans suggests multiple geographic origins.
D.) Neanderthals and other hominid species did not contribute significantly to the human gene pool.

Question #6

The authors of both passages would most likely agree with which of the following statements?

A.) The out-of-Africa model has been entirely disproven by recent genetic research.
B.) The debate over human origins is far from being definitively settled.
C.) The hybridization model provides the only credible explanation for human genetic diversity.
D.) The out-of-Africa model posits that all humans evolved simultaneously across multiple continents.

Question #7

The purpose of the last paragraph in Passage A is to:

A.) Reiterate the author's support for the Out-of-Africa model.
B.) Highlight the drawbacks of the hybridization model.
C.) Discuss the new developments in the study of human origins.
D.) Offer a final conclusive answer to the debate on human origins.

Question #8

The point of view expressed by the author of Passage B towards the Out-of-Africa model can be best described as:

A.) Full endorsement.
B.) Neutral observation.
C.) Open skepticism.
D.) Mild criticism.

***

Reading Passage #3

The artistic community has long debated the merits of traditional art forms versus contemporary ones. Passage A and Passage B present opposing views on the subject.

Passage A

The proponents of traditional art forms argue that they have withstood the test of time, earning their respect and admiration. Traditional art, with its roots deeply embedded in the past, allows us to feel a sense of connection with our ancestors and gain insight into different historical periods. Furthermore, it requires extensive skill and technique honed over many years of dedicated practice. This level of mastery is not often observed in modern forms of art, making traditional art superior.

Passage B

Advocates for contemporary art forms, however, argue that its value lies in its ability to reflect the present and predict the future. Contemporary art can provoke thought, challenge societal norms, and inspire new ideas. The beauty of contemporary art lies not in its technical proficiency but its emotional depth and the social commentary it often provides. It is the art of the present and future, making it more relevant and therefore more valuable.

Question #1

According to Passage A, what differentiates traditional art from contemporary forms?

A.) The emotional depth it provides
B.) Its ability to reflect the present and predict the future
C.) The extensive skill and technique required
D.) Its ability to inspire new ideas

Question #2

According to Passage B, which of the following is a value of contemporary art?

A.) Its ability to connect us with our ancestors
B.) Its reliance on extensive skill and technique
C.) Its ability to provoke thought and challenge societal norms
D.) Its deep roots in the past

Question #3

The authors of both passages would most likely agree with which of the following statements?

A.) The purpose of art is primarily to reflect societal values.
B.) Contemporary art lacks the depth and richness of traditional art.
C.) Both traditional and contemporary art have their own unique values and merits.
D.) Artistic technique is the most crucial aspect of creating valuable art.

Question #4

The tone of Passage A can be described as:

A.) Defiant and antagonistic.
B.) Reverential and appreciative.
C.) Indifferent and detached.
D.) Dismissive and critical.

Question #5

Which statement is supported by both passages?

A.) Contemporary art has no value.
B.) Traditional art is more superior to contemporary art.
C.) Both traditional and contemporary arts have their own values and significance.
D.) The techniques used in traditional art are outdated and no longer relevant.

Question #6

Which statement would the author of Passage B most likely agree with?

A.) Traditional art is irrelevant in today's society.
B.) Contemporary art is the only form of art that should be produced.
C.) The significance of art lies in its ability to challenge societal norms and provoke thought.
D.) The techniques used in traditional art should be forgotten.

Question #7

The author of Passage A would likely disagree with which of the following statements?

A.) Art has the ability to reflect and critique society.
B.) Contemporary art lacks depth and understanding of technique.
C.) The historical context of an artwork is crucial to understanding its significance.
D.) The creative process behind traditional art is formulaic.

Question #8

Based on the information in Passage B, the author would most likely agree with which of the following statements about traditional and contemporary art?

A.) Traditional art is inherently more valuable because of its technical precision.
B.) Contemporary art is a radical break from traditional art and should not be compared.
C.) Both traditional and contemporary art provide unique insights into the human condition.
D.) The advent of contemporary art has led to the devaluation of traditional art forms.

***

Reading Passage #4

Political scientists have long grappled with the influence of political polarization on democratic stability. Traditional theories argued that a moderate level of polarization helps sustain democratic politics by offering voters a clear choice between competing visions for society. However, newer studies suggest that political polarization can undermine democratic stability by making compromise more difficult and encouraging extremist politics. In extreme cases, polarization can even result in political violence or the breakdown of democratic systems.

Although these new theories have empirical support, it is still important to remember that the relationship between political polarization and democratic stability is complex. For instance, some level of polarization may be necessary for democracy because it encourages political engagement and prevents a single party from monopolizing power. Moreover, not all polarization is equivalent: ideological polarization is different from political polarization based on identity, and the latter is often more destructive to democracy.

Question #1

The author of the passage most likely believes that:

A.) Political polarization is the main cause of democratic instability.
B.) Political polarization is a necessary aspect of democracy.
C.) All forms of political polarization are equally harmful to democracy.
D.) The relationship between political polarization and democratic stability is complex and varies depending on the type of polarization.

Question #2

According to the passage, how does political polarization affect democratic stability?

A.) It universally undermines democratic stability.
B.) It only affects democratic stability when it is based on identity.
C.) It can either support or undermine democratic stability, depending on the level and type of polarization.
D.) It has no effect on democratic stability.

Question #3

What can be inferred about identity-based polarization from the passage?

A.) Identity-based polarization is always a threat to democratic stability.
B.) Identity-based polarization can be mitigated by promoting issue-based polarization.
C.) Identity-based polarization is a recent phenomenon.
D.) Identity-based polarization is less predictable and potentially more destructive.

Question #4

According to the passage, why is identity-based polarization considered more destructive than issue-based polarization?

A.) It involves more people.
B.) It often transcends policy disagreements, tapping into personal and group identities.
C.) It makes compromises on policies impossible.
D.) It is a relatively new phenomenon.

Question #5

Which of the following statements, if true, would most strengthen the author's argument?

A.) There is historical evidence that societies with issue-based polarization tend to remain stable for a longer period.
B.) Many psychologists believe that people are more likely to engage in conflicts when their personal identities are involved.
C.) Surveys show that most people don't fully understand policy matters, making issue-based polarization less likely.
D.) An experimental study shows that political polarization is less severe in countries where political discourse is strictly regulated.

Question #6

The author would most likely agree with which of the following statements?

A.) In a politically polarized society, citizens should avoid discussing politics to prevent exacerbating divisions.
B.) Identity-based political polarization is more damaging to societal cohesion than issue-based political polarization.
C.) There is no solution to political polarization; it is a natural consequence of the democratic process.
D.) The best way to combat political polarization is to educate the public on policy matters.

23

Practice Exercise 2

Passage A

The human influence on climate change is undeniable. A majority of scientists agree that human activities, especially the burning of fossil fuels and deforestation, are leading to an increase in the Earth's average temperature. This process, known as global warming, has severe consequences, including extreme weather events, melting ice caps, and rising sea levels. Some people argue that we must reduce our carbon footprint by switching to renewable energy sources and implementing policies that curb deforestation.

Passage B

While human activity undeniably contributes to global warming, the extent of this contribution is often overstated. Natural processes, such as volcanic activity and variations in solar radiation, have a significant impact on the Earth's climate. The belief that human activity is the sole cause of climate change obscures the complexity of the issue. Moreover, the focus on reducing carbon emissions often detracts from other important environmental issues, such as biodiversity loss and habitat destruction.

Question #1

The authors of both passages would most likely agree with which of the following statements?

A.) Human activity is the only cause of climate change.
B.) Global warming has no serious consequences.
C.) Human activity contributes to global warming.
D.) The focus on reducing carbon emissions is unnecessary.

Question #2

How does Passage B primarily differ from Passage A in its approach to the issue of climate change?

A.) Passage B suggests that the impact of human activity on climate change is exaggerated, while Passage A emphasizes the significant role of human activities in causing global warming.

B.) Passage B dismisses the idea of climate change, while Passage A presents evidence to support the idea.

C.) Passage B promotes the use of renewable energy sources, while Passage A highlights the negative effects of using fossil fuels.

D.) Passage B disregards the effects of natural processes on climate change, while Passage A underscores their importance.

Question #3

According to Passage B, why can the focus on reducing carbon emissions be problematic?

A.) It can lead to economic instability.
B.) It may detract from other important environmental issues.
C.) It encourages dependence on fossil fuels.
D.) It can increase the incidence of extreme weather events.

Question #4

Based on Passage A, which one of the following would likely be an effective way to combat global warming?

A.) Implementing policies that curb deforestation
B.) Reducing the occurrence of volcanic activities
C.) Ignoring variations in solar radiation
D.) Promoting biodiversity loss

Question #5

Based on the information in both passages, which of the following statements is most likely to be true?

A.) Policies focusing on reducing carbon emissions are entirely ineffective.
B.) Addressing deforestation can simultaneously combat global warming and biodiversity loss.
C.) Extreme weather events are the primary cause of global warming.
D.) Variations in solar radiation are the leading contributors to global warming.

Question #6

The author's primary purpose in the passage is to:

A) Critique the narrow focus of The Feminine Mystique on middle-class women.
B) Analyze the impact of The Feminine Mystique on the feminist movement.
C) Provide a detailed summary of The Feminine Mystique.
D) Argue that The Feminine Mystique was the most influential feminist work of the 20th century.

***

Reading Passage #2

The United Nations' Declaration of Human Rights, a historic document outlining the inherent and inviolable rights of all individuals, was adopted in 1948 as a response to the atrocities of World War II. The Declaration sought to ensure the preservation of individual dignity and freedom, regardless of nationality, religion, or ethnicity.

Critics of the Declaration, however, have pointed out its shortcomings. It has been argued that it primarily reflects Western values, neglecting the cultural diversity of the global population. Furthermore, its effectiveness has been questioned given that numerous human rights violations occur despite its existence.

Contrastingly, others argue that the universality of the Declaration's principles is its strength. They maintain that the rights outlined in the Declaration are fundamental to humanity and transcend cultural and societal differences. Moreover, they argue, the Declaration's mere existence has an intangible impact: it provides a moral and ethical guideline for nations, influencing their laws and policies.

Question #1

Which of the following statements would the critics of the United Nations' Declaration of Human Rights most likely agree with?

A.) The Declaration should be abandoned as it is ineffective.
B.) The principles of the Declaration are not universal and should be adapted to individual cultures.
C.) The Declaration does not reflect the values of any culture or society.
D.) The atrocities of World War II were not sufficient reasons for the creation of the Declaration.

Question #2

Which of the following statements, if true, would most strengthen the argument of those who support the universality of the Declaration's principles?

A.) A study finds that countries that adhere to the principles of the Declaration have lower rates of human rights violations.
B.) A new international treaty that reflects diverse cultural values has been proposed.
C.) The Declaration has been translated into every language in the world.
D.) A high-profile human rights violation case has recently been highlighted in the media.

Question #3

The author's attitude towards the United Nations' Declaration of Human Rights can best be described as:

A.) Entirely critical.
B.) Entirely supportive.
C.) Balanced, presenting both support and criticism.
D.) Indifferent, with no clear position.

Question #4

The passage suggests which of the following about the effectiveness of the United Nations' Declaration of Human Rights?

A.) It has been completely effective in preventing human rights violations.
B.) Its effectiveness is questioned due to ongoing human rights violations.
C.) It is only effective in Western countries.
D.) It cannot be effective due to cultural differences.

Question #5

The author of the passage would most likely agree with which of the following statements?

A.) The Declaration has been successful in entirely eliminating human rights violations.
B.) The universality of the Declaration's principles are its strength.
C.) The Declaration is entirely ineffective and should be abandoned.
D.) The Declaration reflects only the values of one culture or society.

Question #6

Based on the information in the passage, which of the following can be inferred about the United Nations' Declaration of Human Rights?

A.) It was created as a response to the atrocities of World War I.
B.) It was adopted in the late 19th century.
C.) It outlines the inherent and inviolable rights of all individuals.
D.) It is primarily supported by Western countries.

Question #7

The phrase "profoundly influential" in the context of the passage most likely means:

A.) The declaration has a strong impact on human rights globally.
B.) The declaration has a controversial status.
C.) The declaration has been revised significantly over time.
D.) The declaration has been supported by all nations unanimously.

Question #8

The author's attitude towards the United Nations' Declaration of Human Rights can best be described as:

A.) Adulatory.
B.) Neutral.
C.) Critical.
D.) Confused.

Question #9

Which of the following is NOT presented in the passage as a criticism of the United Nations' Declaration of Human Rights?

A.) It primarily reflects Western values.
B.) It has failed to prevent human rights violations.
C.) It does not recognize the inherent rights of all individuals.
D.) Its principles are too universal to be effective.

* * *

Reading Passage #3

In contemporary society, social media platforms, including Facebook, Twitter, and Instagram, have gained enormous popularity and have significantly influenced how people communicate. These platforms are primarily seen as tools for individuals to connect with friends, family, and other like-minded individuals. However, these platforms are also increasingly becoming mediums for the dissemination of news, ideas, and public debates.

Despite the apparent benefits, critics argue that the rapid propagation of information through social media can often result in the dissemination of false or misleading information, commonly referred to as "fake news." Often, this misinformation is shared more widely and rapidly than verified facts. Some have argued that this phenomenon is a consequence of algorithms used by these platforms, which prioritize content that garners a high level of user engagement, regardless of the truthfulness of the information.

Conversely, proponents of social media argue that the platforms have democratized access to information by reducing reliance on traditional news outlets, which are often controlled by powerful corporations or political entities. Moreover, social media platforms enable the average user to contribute to public discourse and challenge mainstream narratives.

Thus, social media and its role in society present a complex and paradoxical situation. It simultaneously offers the promise of democratized information and the peril of widespread misinformation.

Question #1

According to the passage, which of the following is a primary benefit of social media platforms?

A.) They promote business development.
B.) They connect individuals with their friends, family, and like-minded people.
C.) They provide a platform for advertising and marketing.
D.) They are the most reliable source of information.

Question #2

What is the author's likely opinion about social media's role in the dissemination of news?

A.) It is a positive development as it reduces dependence on traditional news outlets.
B.) It is negative as it leads to the spread of misinformation.
C.) It is a complex phenomenon with both positive and negative aspects.
D.) It should be restricted to personal use and not be used for sharing news.

Question #3

The phrase "democratized access to information" in the context of the passage most likely means:

A.) People have the freedom to access any kind of information they want.
B.) Social media platforms provide equal opportunity for everyone to access and share information.
C.) Traditional news outlets no longer have a monopoly on information.
D.) Social media platforms are governed by democratic principles.

Question #4

Which of the following, if true, would most strengthen the critics' argument about the negative impact of social media on information dissemination?

A.) Social media platforms have stricter content moderation policies than traditional news outlets.
B.) A study found that false information on social media was shared ten times more often than true information.
C.) Social media platforms are more accessible than traditional news outlets.
D.) A significant portion of the global population uses social media.

Question #5

Based on the passage, what is a common argument made by proponents of social media?

A.) Social media platforms should be used strictly for entertainment.
B.) Social media platforms help in better connection with friends and family.
C.) Social media platforms have democratized information by reducing reliance on traditional news outlets.
D.) Social media platforms should be used strictly for personal communication and not for sharing news.

Question #6

According to the passage, which of the following is NOT mentioned as a potential negative consequence of social media?

A.) Increase in the spread of false information.
B.) Overdependence on social media for news.
C.) Decrease in direct, face-to-face communication.
D.) The creation of ideological echo chambers.

Question #7

Which of the following, if true, would most weaken the argument made by proponents of social media?

A.) Traditional news outlets have more rigorous fact-checking processes than social media platforms.
B.) Many people still prefer to get their news from traditional outlets.
C.) False information can still spread on social media even with strict moderation policies.
D.) Social media platforms are often used for non-news related activities.

* * *

Reading Passage #4

The evolutionary history of the dog is a tale that can be traced back millions of years. Dogs are part of the Canidae family, which also includes wolves, foxes, and other extant and extinct species of mammal distinguished by their large canine teeth. While there is consensus that our domesticated dogs are descendants of wolves, the precise path from wild wolf to domesticated dog is much debated among scientists.

One viewpoint suggests that dogs were self-domesticated scavengers that gradually evolved over thousands of years through feeding on the waste of human settlements. However, another theory suggests a more active human role in this process, proposing that humans deliberately tamed and bred wolves for specific roles, such as hunting and guarding.

There is considerable evidence to suggest that the domestication of dogs started around 20,000 to 40,000 years ago, with some archaeological discoveries of buried canine remains alongside human remains dating back 14,000 years. It is often during this era that the physical changes associated with domestication, such as smaller teeth and jaws, become noticeable in canine fossils.

Despite the long history of their domestication, dogs have retained several behavioral traits from their wolf ancestors, such as pack mentality and territoriality. However, selective breeding over generations has led to the wide variety of dog breeds we see today, each with their unique traits and characteristics.

Question #1

According to the passage, which of the following is true about the domestication of dogs?

A.) It occurred around 20,000 to 40,000 years ago.
B.) It is a result of dogs being natural scavengers.
C.) Humans played a minor role in the process.
D.) It led to the disappearance of wolves.

Question #2

Which of the following can be inferred from the passage about the physical changes in dogs due to domestication?

A.) Domesticated dogs have smaller teeth and jaws compared to their wolf ancestors.
B.) Dogs have evolved to have a pack mentality and territoriality.
C.) The physical changes were the result of dogs feeding on human waste.
D.) The physical changes have led to the extinction of some species of the Canidae family.

Question #3

The passage suggests which of the following about the behavioral traits of domesticated dogs?

A.) They have completely lost all behavioral traits of their wolf ancestors.
B.) They have retained some behavioral traits from their wolf ancestors.
C.) They have developed a pack mentality due to living with humans.
D.) Their behavioral traits have nothing in common with their wolf ancestors.

Question #4

What is the author's purpose in the fourth paragraph?

A.) To provide evidence supporting the theory that dogs self-domesticated.
B.) To criticize the theory that humans played a significant role in dog domestication.
C.) To detail the time frame and physical changes associated with dog domestication.
D.) To argue that domesticated dogs and wolves are completely different species.

Question #5

According to the passage, which of the following best explains the term 'self-domestication' in the context of dog domestication?

A.) Dogs adapted to live among humans without direct human intervention.
B.) Humans actively bred dogs to promote desirable traits.
C.) Wolves voluntarily joined human communities and became dogs.
D.) Dogs chose to domesticate other animals in their vicinity.

Question #6

The author uses the phrase "a bone of contention" in line 3 most likely to:

A.) Indicate the skeletal evidence that supports dog domestication theories.
B.) Refer to the physical changes dogs underwent during domestication.
C.) Suggest a point of disagreement or debate regarding dog domestication.
D.) Highlight the importance of bones in the diet of ancient dogs.

24

Practice Exercise 1: Answers and Explanations

Reading Passage 1

Question #1

Question #1 - Correct Answer and Explanations

C.) The Feminine Mystique challenged traditional gender roles and sparked a societal shift in attitudes toward women's roles.

Explanation: This is the correct answer because it most accurately summarizes the main idea of the passage. The passage discusses the impact of The Feminine Mystique, including its critique of gender roles and its call for women to seek fulfillment outside these roles. It also highlights the book's influence on societal attitudes and the feminist movement.

Question #1 - Wrong Answer Explanations:

A.) The Feminine Mystique was a flawed book that overlooked the experiences of many women.

Explanation: While the passage acknowledges criticism of The Feminine Mystique for its focus on the experiences of white, middle-class women, it does not identify this as the main idea. The criticism is presented as a limitation, but not as the central focus of the book or the passage.

B.) Betty Friedan was a key figure in the second-wave feminist movement.

Explanation: While this statement is true and is supported by the passage, it is not the main idea of the passage. The primary focus is on the impact and limitations of The Feminine Mystique, not specifically on Betty Friedan's role in the feminist movement.

D.) The Feminine Mystique was solely a critique of society's prescribed gender roles.

Explanation: This answer is incorrect because it overlooks a significant part of the passage's discussion of The Feminine Mystique. While the book does critique society's prescribed gender roles, the passage also emphasizes that it calls for women to seek fulfillment outside these roles and discusses its influence on societal attitudes and the feminist movement.

Question #2

Correct Answer and Explanations

C.) The Feminine Mystique contributed to the onset of the second-wave feminist movement.

Explanation: This statement is correct and is supported by the passage. The last sentence of the passage directly states that Friedan's work "served as a catalyst for the second-wave feminist movement."

Question #2 - Wrong Answer Explanations:

A.) Betty Friedan was critical of the feminist movement.

Explanation: The passage does not provide any information to suggest that Friedan was critical of the feminist movement. Rather, she is presented as a significant figure within the movement.

B.) The Feminine Mystique primarily addressed the needs of marginalized groups.

Explanation: This answer is incorrect. In fact, the passage states the opposite - that one of the main criticisms of The Feminine Mystique was its focus on the experiences of white, middle-class women and its neglect of the experiences of marginalized groups.

D.) Betty Friedan believed that a woman's worth was solely tied to her role as a homemaker.

Explanation: This answer contradicts the information in the passage. According to the passage, Friedan argued against the idea that a woman's worth was tied to her role as a homemaker, instead advocating for women to seek personal fulfillment and societal value outside of these traditional roles.

Question #3

Correct Answer and Explanations

C.) Friedan played a crucial role in raising awareness about the issues faced by women in the mid-20th century America.

Explanation: This answer aligns with the overall tone and content of the passage. The author acknowledges Friedan's significant contribution to the second-wave feminist movement and her influence in challenging societal norms related to women's roles.

Question #3 - Wrong Answer Explanations:

A.) Friedan's emphasis on the plight of middle-class women undermined the broader goals of the feminist movement.

Explanation: While the passage notes some criticism of Friedan's focus on middle-class women, it does not suggest that this focus undermined the broader goals of the feminist movement.

B.) Friedan's arguments in "The Feminine Mystique" were universally accepted by all women at the time of its publication.

Explanation: The passage doesn't provide any information suggesting that Friedan's arguments were universally accepted by all women. Rather, the passage indicates there was some criticism for its narrow focus.

D.) Friedan's writing was primarily inspired by her experiences as a marginalized woman.

Explanation: The passage does not provide any information to support the idea that Friedan's personal experiences as a marginalized woman directly influenced her writing. The only suggestion of her personal experience is that she was dissatisfied with the societal expectations placed on women.

Question #4

Correct Answer and Explanations

B.) Analyze the impact of "The Feminine Mystique" on the feminist movement in the 1960s.

Explanation: The primary aim of the passage is to analyze the impact that Friedan's work, specifically "The Feminine Mystique", had on the feminist movement. The passage discusses the effects of the book on society and how it influenced women's roles and contributed to the initiation of the second-wave feminist movement.

Question #4 - Wrong Answer Explanations:

A.) Criticize Betty Friedan for her focus on middle-class women in "The Feminine Mystique".

Explanation: The passage does mention that there was criticism of Friedan's focus on middle-class women, but this is not the primary purpose of the passage. The overall tone is more analytical than critical, and the author seems to regard Friedan's work as an essential element of the second-wave feminist movement.

C.) Argue that "The Feminine Mystique" was the sole cause of the second-wave feminist movement.

Explanation: The passage emphasizes the influence of "The Feminine Mystique" in catalyzing the second-wave feminist movement, but it does not claim that it was the sole cause of the movement.

D.) Offer a tribute to Betty Friedan for her contributions to the women's movement.

Explanation: Although the passage acknowledges Friedan's significant contributions to the women's movement, its primary purpose is more analytical than celebratory, as it examines the societal impact and reception of "The Feminine Mystique".

Question #5

Correct Answer and Explanations

D.) The Feminine Mystique played a crucial role in stimulating dialogue about women's societal roles.

Explanation: This assertion aligns with the author's analysis of the impact of "The Feminine Mystique." The author acknowledges the book as a pivotal influence that catalyzed significant societal dialogue and changes regarding women's roles, despite some criticism.

Question #5 - Wrong Answer Explanations:

A.) The Feminine Mystique was universally praised upon its release.

Explanation: The author explicitly acknowledges in the passage that Friedan's work received criticism for its focus on middle-class women, which contradicts this statement.

B.) Friedan's focus on middle-class women was a significant flaw in her work.

Explanation: While the author mentions that some critics held this view, the author does not personally endorse it. The passage predominantly emphasizes the book's overall positive impact on the feminist movement.

C.) The Feminine Mystique did more harm than good in advancing the cause of feminism.

Explanation: This viewpoint is not supported by the passage. The author consistently characterizes "The Feminine Mystique" as a key instigator of the second-wave feminist movement, despite acknowledging some criticism of its limited focus.

Question #6

Correct Answer and Explanations

B.) Analyze the impact of The Feminine Mystique on the feminist movement.

Explanation: The author's main purpose is to discuss how The Feminine Mystique influenced the feminist movement, regardless of criticisms of its scope. The author gives a balanced perspective, noting both the criticisms and the positive effects of Friedan's work.

Question #6 - Wrong Answer Explanations:

A.) Critique the narrow focus of The Feminine Mystique on middle-class women.

Explanation: While the author does acknowledge the critique of Friedan's focus on middle-class women, this is not the primary purpose of the passage. The author's main aim is to evaluate the overall impact of The Feminine Mystique, both positive and negative.

C.) Provide a detailed summary of The Feminine Mystique.

Explanation: Although the author discusses the themes and criticisms of The Feminine Mystique, the passage does not provide a detailed summary of the book. Rather, the focus is more on the influence of the book on societal perceptions of women's roles.

D.) Argue that The Feminine Mystique was the most influential feminist work of the 20th century.

Explanation: Although the author acknowledges the book's significant influence on the feminist movement, they do not make a claim that it was the most influential feminist work of the 20th century.

***

Reading Passage #2

Question #1

Correct Answer and Explanations

B.) Passage B extends an idea presented in Passage A.

Explanation: Passage A discusses the uniqueness of Neanderthals and suggests they may be a separate species from Homo sapiens. Passage B extends this idea by acknowledging their uniqueness, but also discussing evidence of interbreeding between Neanderthals and Homo sapiens.

Question #1 - Wrong Answer Explanations:

A.) Passage B disputes a claim made in Passage A.

Explanation: Passage B does not dispute the claims made in Passage A; rather, it adds to the discussion by introducing genetic evidence of interbreeding.

C.) Passage B contradicts the conclusion drawn in Passage A.

Explanation: Passage B does not contradict the conclusion in Passage A. Passage A suggests that Neanderthals might be a separate species, and Passage B does not dispute this. Instead, it adds that there was interbreeding between the two species.

D.) Passage A and Passage B discuss different aspects of the same topic.

Explanation: While it is true that the passages are discussing different aspects of the same topic, this is not the best answer because Passage B directly extends the idea presented in Passage A, which is a more precise characterization of the relationship.

Question #2

Correct Answer and Explanations

C.) It underscores the complexity of human evolution.

Explanation: Passage B states that the discovery of Neanderthal DNA in present-day non-African humans "challenges the notion of a pure lineage of Homo sapiens, and underlines the complexity of human evolution," which matches best with answer choice C.

Question #2 - Wrong Answer Explanations:

A.) It supports the notion that Neanderthals were a separate species.

Explanation: The discovery of Neanderthal DNA in non-African humans does not necessarily support the idea that Neanderthals were a separate species. It suggests interbreeding, which complicates the species distinction.

B.) It validates the linear model of human evolution.

Explanation: The presence of Neanderthal DNA actually challenges the linear model of evolution by suggesting a more complex, branching model.

D.) It proves that Homo sapiens migrated out of Africa.

Explanation: While the passage does mention Homo sapiens migrating out of Africa, the discovery of Neanderthal DNA in non-African humans is not presented as proof of this migration. Rather, it's presented as evidence of interbreeding between species.

Question #3

Correct Answer and Explanations

D.) Passage A supports the out-of-Africa model while Passage B argues for a hybrid model of human evolution.

Explanation: Passage A presents a view that aligns with the out-of-Africa model, describing a migration of Homo sapiens from Africa that replaced local hominid populations. On the other hand, Passage B presents evidence suggesting a more complex, hybrid model where interbreeding occurred between species, complicating the simple linear or out-of-Africa models.

Question #3 - Wrong Answer Explanations:

A.) Passage A believes in the multiregional model while Passage B supports the out-of-Africa model.

Explanation: The multiregional model is not mentioned in either passage, and Passage A, not B, supports the out-of-Africa model.

B.) Passage A advocates for the linear model while Passage B suggests a branching model.

Explanation: While Passage B does suggest a more complex model that could be interpreted as branching, Passage A does not explicitly advocate for a linear model of evolution.

C.) Passage A views Neanderthals as a distinct species, while Passage B views them as a sub-species of Homo sapiens.

Explanation: Neither passage makes a clear claim about whether Neanderthals are a distinct species or a sub-species of Homo sapiens.

Question #4

Correct Answer and Explanations

C.) Passage A suggests that the Neanderthals were completely replaced by Homo sapiens.

Explanation: Passage A supports the out-of-Africa model, which proposes that Homo sapiens emerged from Africa and replaced local hominid populations, including Neanderthals.

Question #4 - Wrong Answer Explanations:

A.) Both passages explicitly support the out-of-Africa model of human evolution.

Explanation: Only Passage A supports the out-of-Africa model, while Passage B presents a more complex, hybrid model of human evolution.

B.) Passage B disagrees with the idea of interbreeding among hominid species.

Explanation: Passage B actually provides evidence supporting the idea of interbreeding among hominid species, suggesting a hybrid model of human evolution.

D.) Both passages argue that the multiregional model of human evolution is the most accurate.

Explanation: Neither passage supports the multiregional model. Passage A supports the out-of-Africa model, and Passage B suggests a hybrid model of human evolution.

Question #5

Correct Answer and Explanations

D.) Neanderthals and other hominid species did not contribute significantly to the human gene pool.

Explanation: Passage A suggests that the out-of-Africa model asserts Homo sapiens emerged from Africa and replaced local hominid populations. This suggests that, according to this model, other hominid species did not contribute significantly to the human gene pool.

Question #5 - Wrong Answer Explanations:

A.) Interbreeding between hominid species was an uncommon occurrence.

Explanation: This statement does not explicitly align with the out-of-Africa model as described in Passage A.

B.) Homo sapiens have genetic traces of other hominid species, such as Neanderthals.

Explanation: This assertion is more in line with the hybrid model as discussed in Passage B, which allows for interbreeding and genetic contributions from other hominid species.

C.) The genetic diversity among modern humans suggests multiple geographic origins.

Explanation: This statement is contrary to the out-of-Africa model presented in Passage A, which posits a single geographic origin for modern humans.

Question #6

Correct Answer and Explanations

B.) The debate over human origins is far from being definitively settled.

Explanation: Both Passage A and B acknowledge that the debate on human origins is ongoing. Passage A concludes by stating that the debate "continues to evolve," while Passage B notes that the hybridization model has "challenged" the established view without fully displacing it.

Question #6 - Wrong Answer Explanations:

A.) The out-of-Africa model has been entirely disproven by recent genetic research.

Explanation: While the hybridization model challenged the out-of-Africa model, neither passage claims that the out-of-Africa model has been entirely disproven.

C.) The hybridization model provides the only credible explanation for human genetic diversity.

Explanation: Passage B presents the hybridization model as a compelling alternative, but neither passage asserts it as the only credible explanation.

D.) The out-of-Africa model posits that all humans evolved simultaneously across multiple continents.

Explanation: This statement contradicts Passage A's description of the out-of-Africa model, which posits a single African origin for Homo sapiens.

Question #7

Correct Answer and Explanations

C.) Discuss the new developments in the study of human origins.

Explanation: The last paragraph in Passage A talks about the new developments such as the discovery of Denisovans and Neanderthals, and the further evolution of the debate on human origins.

Question #7 - Wrong Answer Explanations:

A.) Reiterate the author's support for the Out-of-Africa model.

Explanation: The last paragraph doesn't reiterate any support for the Out-of-Africa model, instead it talks about new developments that have challenged this model.

B.) Highlight the drawbacks of the hybridization model.

Explanation: The last paragraph doesn't discuss any drawbacks of the hybridization model. It mentions this model only in the context of new developments in the study of human origins.

D.) Offer a final conclusive answer to the debate on human origins.

Explanation: The last paragraph doesn't offer a conclusive answer to the debate, but instead indicates that the debate "continues to evolve" with new developments.

Question #8

Correct Answer and Explanations

D.) Mild criticism.

Explanation: The author of Passage B provides a balanced view of the debate between the Out-of-Africa model and the hybridization model but does express mild criticism of the Out-of-Africa model by stating that it "oversimplifies the complexities of human evolution" and is "an incomplete account at best."

Question #8 - Wrong Answer Explanations:

A.) Full endorsement.

Explanation: The author of Passage B doesn't fully endorse the Out-of-Africa model. Instead, they express some criticism towards it, making this option incorrect.

B.) Neutral observation.

Explanation: While the author of Passage B presents both the Out-of-Africa model and the hybridization model, they express some criticism of the former. Thus, their perspective cannot be considered as purely neutral.

C.) Open skepticism.

Explanation: Although the author of Passage B criticizes the Out-of-Africa model to some extent, they do not dismiss it outright or express open skepticism. They acknowledge that it has its merits but state that it is an "incomplete account at best". Therefore, this option is not correct.

**

Reading Passage #3

Question #1

Correct Answer and Explanations

C.) The extensive skill and technique required

Explanation: Passage A argues that traditional art forms require "extensive skill and technique honed over many years of dedicated practice." This aspect is stated to be lacking in contemporary art forms, differentiating the two.

Question #1 - Wrong Answer Explanations:

A.) The emotional depth it provides

Explanation: While emotional depth might be a part of traditional art, it is not mentioned as a differentiating factor in Passage A. On the contrary, emotional depth is identified in Passage B as a characteristic of contemporary art.

B.) Its ability to reflect the present and predict the future

Explanation: The ability to reflect the present and predict the future is described in Passage B as a characteristic of contemporary art, not traditional art.

D.) Its ability to inspire new ideas

Explanation: The ability to inspire new ideas is highlighted in Passage B as a feature of contemporary art, not traditional art.

Question #2

Correct Answer and Explanations

C.) Its ability to provoke thought and challenge societal norms

Explanation: Passage B argues that the value of contemporary art lies in its "ability to provoke thought, challenge societal norms, and inspire new ideas." Therefore, choice (C) accurately reflects the view presented in the passage.

Question #2 - Wrong Answer Explanations:

A.) Its ability to connect us with our ancestors

Explanation: This is mentioned as a value of traditional art in Passage A. Passage B does not attribute this quality to contemporary art.

B.) Its reliance on extensive skill and technique

Explanation: This characteristic is associated with traditional art according to Passage A. Passage B does not highlight this as a characteristic of contemporary art.

D.) Its deep roots in the past

Explanation: This characteristic is associated with traditional art as per Passage A. Passage B does not mention this as a characteristic of contemporary art. In fact, it portrays contemporary art as reflecting the present and predicting the future.

Question #3

Correct Answer and Explanations

C.) Both traditional and contemporary art have their own unique values and merits.

Explanation: Both authors, despite their different focus, acknowledge the importance and value of both traditional and contemporary art, albeit emphasizing different aspects.

Question #3 - Wrong Answer Explanations:

A.) The purpose of art is primarily to reflect societal values.

Explanation: While this might be inferred from Passage B's discussion of contemporary art, Passage A does not necessarily concur, instead focusing more on the idea of art as a connection to the past and a demonstration of skill and technique.

B.) Contemporary art lacks the depth and richness of traditional art.

Explanation: This is contrary to the views expressed in Passage B, which emphasizes the power of contemporary art to provoke thought and challenge societal norms. Passage A does not directly devalue contemporary art.

D.) Artistic technique is the most crucial aspect of creating valuable art.

Explanation: While Passage A emphasizes the importance of technique in traditional art, Passage B downplays the role of technique in favor of the ability of art to provoke thought and challenge societal norms. Therefore, the authors would not agree that technique is the most crucial aspect of valuable art.

Question #4

Correct Answer and Explanations

B.) Reverential and appreciative.

Explanation: Passage A reveres traditional art, appreciating its technique, the skill required, and the connection to the past it represents. There's no sense of defiance, antagonism, indifference, or dismissiveness in the author's attitude towards traditional art.

Question #4 - Wrong Answer Explanations:

A.) Defiant and antagonistic.

Explanation: Passage A doesn't express defiance or antagonism; instead, the author expresses appreciation for traditional art without arguing against other perspectives or ideas.

C.) Indifferent and detached.

Explanation: The author of Passage A demonstrates a deep appreciation and passion for traditional art, contradicting any suggestion of indifference or detachment.

D.) Dismissive and critical.

Explanation: While the author of Passage A does not place as much value on contemporary art as traditional art, they do not dismiss or criticize it, but instead focus on explaining why traditional art holds a specific value for them.

Question #5

Correct Answer and Explanations

C.) Both traditional and contemporary arts have their own values and significance.

Explanation: Both passages acknowledge the values inherent in both traditional and contemporary art, albeit in different ways. Passage A appreciates the skills and connection to the past that traditional art offers while recognizing the freedom in contemporary art. Passage B sees value in contemporary art's ability to provoke thought and challenge norms but doesn't dismiss the importance of traditional art.

Question #5 - Wrong Answer Explanations:

A.) Contemporary art has no value.

Explanation: Passage A might focus on the value of traditional art, but it doesn't state that contemporary art has no value. Passage B explicitly appreciates contemporary art's value.

B.) Traditional art is more superior to contemporary art.

Explanation: Neither passage explicitly states that traditional art is superior. Passage A prefers traditional art, while Passage B prefers contemporary art, but both acknowledge the value of the other.

D.) The techniques used in traditional art are outdated and no longer relevant.

Explanation: Passage B might argue that contemporary art can offer more freedom, but it doesn't state that the techniques of traditional art are outdated or irrelevant. Passage A, on the other hand, appreciates the techniques of traditional art.

Question #6

Correct Answer and Explanations

C.) The significance of art lies in its ability to challenge societal norms and provoke thought.

Explanation: Passage B clearly appreciates contemporary art's ability to challenge societal norms and provoke thought, stating that it has the "ability to provoke, challenge, and confront." This aligns with the idea that the significance of art lies in its thought-provoking capabilities.

Question #6 - Wrong Answer Explanations:

A.) Traditional art is irrelevant in today's society.

Explanation: While the author of Passage B appreciates contemporary art, they do not dismiss the relevance of traditional art. They acknowledge traditional art but prefer the freedom and challenge contemporary art provides.

B.) Contemporary art is the only form of art that should be produced.

Explanation: The author of Passage B praises contemporary art but does not suggest that it should be the only form of art produced. They acknowledge the place and importance of traditional art.

D.) The techniques used in traditional art should be forgotten.

Explanation: The author of Passage B appreciates the freedom of contemporary art but does not explicitly suggest that the techniques of traditional art should be forgotten. They acknowledge that both forms of art have their place.

Question #7

Correct Answer and Explanations

B.) Contemporary art lacks depth and understanding of technique.

Explanation: The author of Passage A appreciates both traditional and contemporary art. While they celebrate the technical mastery of traditional art, they also acknowledge the depth and value in contemporary art, making it unlikely that they would agree with the statement that contemporary art lacks depth and understanding of technique.

Question #7 - Wrong Answer Explanations:

A.) Art has the ability to reflect and critique society.

Explanation: The author of Passage A recognizes that art, including contemporary art, can reflect society's complexities and act as a critique, making it unlikely that they would disagree with this statement.

C.) The historical context of an artwork is crucial to understanding its significance.

Explanation: The author of Passage A indicates an appreciation for the historical context and mastery of technique in traditional art, making it unlikely that they would disagree with the assertion that the historical context of artwork is crucial.

D.) The creative process behind traditional art is formulaic.

Explanation: The author of Passage A expresses an admiration for the technical mastery and creative process of traditional art, and there is no evidence in the passage to suggest that they would view this process as formulaic.

Question #8

Correct Answer and Explanations

C.) Both traditional and contemporary art provide unique insights into the human condition.

Explanation: The author of Passage B seems to place equal value on both traditional and contemporary art. They see the value in the precision of traditional art and also appreciate the boldness and innovation of contemporary art, seeing both as capable of providing unique insights into the human condition.

Question #8 - Wrong Answer Explanations:

A.) Traditional art is inherently more valuable because of its technical precision.

Explanation: While the author acknowledges the technical precision of traditional art, they don't state that this makes it more valuable. In fact, they value both forms of art for their unique contributions.

B.) Contemporary art is a radical break from traditional art and should not be compared.

Explanation: The author does not argue for a complete separation of traditional and contemporary art. Rather, they appreciate the links and differences between them, and believe that both can provide valuable insights.

D.) The advent of contemporary art has led to the devaluation of traditional art forms.

Explanation: The author does not suggest that the rise of contemporary art has caused traditional art to be devalued. They appreciate the precision of traditional art and the boldness of contemporary art, suggesting a valuation of both forms.

***

Reading Passage #4

Question #1

Correct Answer and Explanations

D.) The relationship between political polarization and democratic stability is complex and varies depending on the type of polarization.

Explanation: The passage states that "the relationship between political polarization and democratic stability is complex" and "not all polarization is equivalent." This clearly aligns with option D.

Question #1 - Wrong Answer Explanations:

A.) Political polarization is the main cause of democratic instability.

Explanation: The passage suggests that polarization can contribute to democratic instability, but it does not claim that it is the main cause.

B.) Political polarization is a necessary aspect of democracy.

Explanation: While the passage does state that "some level of polarization may be necessary for democracy," it does not posit that it is a necessary aspect overall, making this choice incorrect.

C.) All forms of political polarization are equally harmful to democracy.

Explanation: The passage explicitly states that "not all polarization is equivalent: ideological polarization is different from political polarization based on identity, and the latter is often more destructive to democracy." Therefore, the author does not believe that all forms of polarization are equally harmful.

Question #2

Correct Answer and Explanations

C.) It can either support or undermine democratic stability, depending on the level and type of polarization.

Explanation: The passage discusses how moderate polarization can provide clear choices for voters and prevent monopolization of power, potentially supporting democratic stability. However, it also mentions that extreme polarization can result in political violence and breakdown of democratic systems, undermining stability. Additionally, the author notes that the type of polarization also matters, with identity-based polarization often being more destructive.

Question #2 - Wrong Answer Explanations:

A.) It universally undermines democratic stability.

Explanation: The passage notes both positive and negative effects of polarization on democratic stability, not just negative ones.

B.) It only affects democratic stability when it is based on identity.

Explanation: The passage does mention that identity-based polarization can be particularly harmful, but it doesn't state that polarization only affects democratic stability when it is based on identity.

D.) It has no effect on democratic stability.

Explanation: The passage clearly outlines various ways in which political polarization does affect democratic stability, making this option incorrect.

Question #3

Correct Answer and Explanations

D.) Identity-based polarization is less predictable and potentially more destructive.

Explanation: The passage specifically states that identity-based polarization tends to be "less predictable and potentially more destructive." This is because it can result in conflicts that go beyond policy disagreements, entering into the territory of personal and group identities.

Question #3 - Wrong Answer Explanations:

A.) Identity-based polarization is always a threat to democratic stability.

Explanation: While the passage does state that identity-based polarization can be harmful, it does not categorically claim that it always threatens democratic stability.

B.) Identity-based polarization can be mitigated by promoting issue-based polarization.

Explanation: The passage does not provide any information to suggest that issue-based polarization can be used as a countermeasure against identity-based polarization.

C.) Identity-based polarization is a recent phenomenon.

Explanation: The passage does not specify when identity-based polarization began or suggest that it is a recent development.

Question #4

Correct Answer and Explanations

B.) It often transcends policy disagreements, tapping into personal and group identities.

Explanation: The passage indicates that identity-based polarization is considered more destructive than issue-based polarization because it can tap into personal and group identities, which tends to be less predictable and potentially more destructive. It does not merely hinge on policy disagreements, but rather transcends them.

Question #4- Wrong Answer Explanations:

A.) It involves more people.

Explanation: The passage does not provide any information to suggest that identity-based polarization involves more people than issue-based polarization.

C.) It makes compromises on policies impossible.

Explanation: While the passage implies that identity-based polarization can make policy disagreements more contentious, it does not go as far as to claim that it makes policy compromises impossible.

D.) It is a relatively new phenomenon.

Explanation: The passage does not discuss the temporal aspects of identity-based polarization, so there is no basis for claiming that it is a new phenomenon.

Question #5

Correct Answer and Explanations

B.) Many psychologists believe that people are more likely to engage in conflicts when their personal identities are involved.

Explanation: The author's argument centers on the idea that identity-based polarization is more destructive than issue-based polarization because it taps into personal and group identities. If psychologists generally believe that involvement of personal identities increases the likelihood of conflict, this would strengthen the author's argument.

Question #5- Wrong Answer Explanations:

A.) There is historical evidence that societies with issue-based polarization tend to remain stable for a longer period.

Explanation: While this statement, if true, might indirectly suggest that identity-based polarization is more destructive, it doesn't directly support the author's argument about the impact of involving personal and group identities in political polarization.

C.) Surveys show that most people don't fully understand policy matters, making issue-based polarization less likely.

Explanation: This statement, while potentially explaining why issue-based polarization might be less prevalent, does not add to the author's argument about why identity-based polarization is more destructive.

D.) An experimental study shows that political polarization is less severe in countries where political discourse is strictly regulated.

Explanation: The author's argument doesn't involve the regulation of political discourse, so this statement doesn't directly strengthen it. It might be relevant to a broader discussion of polarization, but it doesn't specifically bolster the author's argument about identity-based versus issue-based polarization.

Question #6

Correct Answer and Explanations

B.) Identity-based political polarization is more damaging to societal cohesion than issue-based political polarization.

Explanation: This statement aligns with the author's central argument in the passage, which is that identity-based political polarization, not issue-based polarization, is more detrimental to a society.

Question #6- Wrong Answer Explanations:

A.) In a politically polarized society, citizens should avoid discussing politics to prevent exacerbating divisions.

Explanation: This option is incorrect because the passage does not discuss whether citizens should avoid discussing politics. The focus is on the type of polarization, not the avoidance of political discussion.

C.) There is no solution to political polarization; it is a natural consequence of the democratic process.

Explanation: The passage does not state or imply that there is no solution to political polarization. The author discusses the differences between types of polarization but does not assert that it is a natural or unavoidable consequence of democracy.

D.) The best way to combat political polarization is to educate the public on policy matters.

Explanation: While this may be a possible solution to combat polarization, the passage does not mention this specific method. The author focuses on comparing two types of polarization and their effects on society.

***

25

Practice Exercise 2: Answers and Explanations

Reading Passage #1

Question #1

Correct Answer and Explanations

C.) Human activity contributes to global warming.

Explanation: Both authors acknowledge that human activity contributes to global warming, despite their differences in emphasis on its extent.

Question #1 - Wrong Answer Explanations:

A.) Human activity is the only cause of climate change.

Explanation: Passage B specifically argues against the notion that human activity is the sole cause of climate change, which contradicts this choice.

B.) Global warming has no serious consequences.

Explanation: Both passages acknowledge the serious consequences of global warming.

D.) The focus on reducing carbon emissions is unnecessary.

Explanation: Passage A promotes reducing our carbon footprint, while Passage B does not explicitly state that reducing carbon emissions is unnecessary, only that it can detract from other environmental issues.

Question #2

Correct Answer and Explanations

A.) Passage B suggests that the impact of human activity on climate change is exaggerated, while Passage A emphasizes the significant role of human activities in causing global warming.

Explanation: Passage A emphasizes the significant role of human activities in causing global warming, while Passage B suggests that the impact of human activity on climate change is often overstated.

Question #2 - Wrong Answer Explanations:

B.) Passage B dismisses the idea of climate change, while Passage A presents evidence to support the idea.

Explanation: Neither passage dismisses the idea of climate change.

C.) Passage B promotes the use of renewable energy sources, while Passage A highlights the negative effects of using fossil fuels.

Explanation: Passage B does not promote the use of renewable energy sources.

D.) Passage B disregards the effects of natural processes on climate change, while Passage A underscores their importance.

Explanation: Passage B does not disregard the effects of natural processes on climate change. In fact, it argues that these processes significantly impact the Earth's climate.

Question #3

Correct Answer and Explanations

B.) It may detract from other important environmental issues.

Explanation: Passage B mentions that the focus on reducing carbon emissions can detract from other important environmental issues such as biodiversity loss and habitat destruction.

Question #3 - Wrong Answer Explanations:

A.) It can lead to economic instability.

Explanation: Passage B does not discuss the potential economic impact of focusing on reducing carbon emissions.

C.) It encourages dependence on fossil fuels.

Explanation: Passage B does not suggest that focusing on reducing carbon emissions encourages dependence on fossil fuels.

D.) It can increase the incidence of extreme weather events.

Explanation: Passage B does not imply that focusing on reducing carbon emissions can increase the incidence of extreme weather events.

Question #4

Correct Answer and Explanations

A.) Implementing policies that curb deforestation.

Explanation: Passage A states that policies that curb deforestation can help reduce our carbon footprint, implying that this could be an effective way to combat global warming.

Question #4 - Wrong Answer Explanations:

B.) Reducing the occurrence of volcanic activities.

Explanation: Passage A does not discuss reducing the occurrence of volcanic activities as a solution to global warming.

C.) Ignoring variations in solar radiation.

Explanation: Ignoring variations in solar radiation is not suggested as a solution to global warming in Passage A.

D.) Promoting biodiversity loss.

Explanation: Passage A does not suggest promoting biodiversity loss as a solution to global warming. In fact, biodiversity loss is typically viewed as a negative environmental outcome.

Question #5

Correct Answer and Explanations

B.) Addressing deforestation can simultaneously combat global warming and biodiversity loss.

Explanation: Passage A mentions that curbing deforestation can help reduce our carbon footprint and therefore combat global warming. Passage B mentions that focusing solely on carbon emissions can detract from other important environmental issues like biodiversity loss, implying that a more comprehensive approach, such as addressing deforestation, can simultaneously combat both issues.

Question #5 - Wrong Answer Explanations:

A.) Policies focusing on reducing carbon emissions are entirely ineffective.

Explanation: Neither passage suggests that policies focusing on reducing carbon emissions are entirely ineffective.

C.) Extreme weather events are the primary cause of global warming.

Explanation: Neither passage identifies extreme weather events as the primary cause of global warming.

D.) Variations in solar radiation are the leading contributors to global warming.

Explanation: Neither passage suggests that variations in solar radiation are the leading contributors to global warming.

Question #6

Correct Answer and Explanations

B.) Global warming is an issue that requires a multifaceted approach.

Explanation: Both passages suggest that global warming is a complex issue that cannot be solved by addressing carbon emissions alone. Passage A suggests that policies to curb deforestation can help reduce our carbon footprint, while Passage B argues for a more comprehensive approach to environmental issues, suggesting that the authors would agree with the need for a multifaceted approach to global warming.

Question #6 - Wrong Answer Explanations:

A.) Carbon emissions are the sole cause of global warming.

Explanation: Neither passage suggests that carbon emissions are the sole cause of global warming.

C.) Biodiversity loss has no significant impact on global warming.

Explanation: Passage B specifically mentions biodiversity loss as an important environmental issue that can be overlooked when the focus is solely on reducing carbon emissions.

D.) Deforestation has no significant role in global warming.

Explanation: Passage A discusses the role of deforestation in contributing to global warming, suggesting that it plays a significant role.

* * *

Reading Passage #2

Question #1

Correct Answer and Explanations

B.) The principles of the Declaration are not universal and should be adapted to individual cultures.

Explanation: The passage mentions that critics argue that the Declaration primarily reflects Western values and neglects the cultural diversity of the global population, suggesting that these critics might believe that the Declaration's principles are not universal and should be adapted to individual cultures.

Question #1 - Wrong Answer Explanations:

A.) The Declaration should be abandoned as it is ineffective.

Explanation: Critics of the Declaration question its effectiveness but the passage does not suggest that they believe it should be abandoned.

C.) The Declaration does not reflect the values of any culture or society.

Explanation: Critics argue that the Declaration reflects primarily Western values, not that it doesn't reflect any culture or society.

D.) The atrocities of World War II were not sufficient reasons for the creation of the Declaration.

Explanation: The passage does not mention critics' views on the reasons for the creation of the Declaration.

Question #2

Correct Answer and Explanations

A.) A study finds that countries that adhere to the principles of the Declaration have lower rates of human rights violations.

Explanation: This statement directly supports the argument that the Declaration's principles are universally applicable and effective, therefore strengthening the argument of those who support its universality.

Question #2 - Wrong Answer Explanations:

B.) A new international treaty that reflects diverse cultural values has been proposed.

Explanation: This statement is irrelevant to the argument of those who support the universality of the Declaration's principles.

C.) The Declaration has been translated into every language in the world.

Explanation: The number of languages into which the Declaration has been translated does not necessarily strengthen the argument of those who support its universality.

D.) A high-profile human rights violation case has recently been highlighted in the media.

Explanation: This statement is unrelated to the universality of the Declaration's principles.

Question #3

Correct Answer and Explanations

C.) Balanced, presenting both support and criticism.

Explanation: The author presents both criticisms of the Declaration (it primarily reflects Western values and its effectiveness is questionable) and arguments in its support (the universality of its principles and its intangible impact as a moral and ethical guideline), indicating a balanced view.

Question #3 - Wrong Answer Explanations:

A.) Entirely critical.

Explanation: The author is not entirely critical, as they also present arguments in support of the Declaration.

B.) Entirely supportive.

Explanation: The author is not entirely supportive, as they also present criticisms of the Declaration.

D.) Indifferent, with no clear position.

Explanation: The author shows interest in the topic by discussing both criticisms and support for the Declaration, indicating that they are not indifferent.

Question #4

Correct Answer and Explanations

B.) Its effectiveness is questioned due to ongoing human rights violations.

Explanation: The passage mentions that critics have questioned the effectiveness of the Declaration given that human rights violations continue to occur.

Question #4 - Wrong Answer Explanations:

A.) It has been completely effective in preventing human rights violations.

Explanation: The passage clearly states that the Declaration's effectiveness is questioned, suggesting it has not been completely effective.

C.) It is only effective in Western countries.

Explanation: The passage does not suggest that the Declaration is only effective in Western countries.

D.) It cannot be effective due to cultural differences.

Explanation: The passage does not suggest that the Declaration cannot be effective due to cultural differences.

Question #5

Correct Answer and Explanations

B.) The universality of the Declaration's principles are its strength.

Explanation: The author presents this point as part of the arguments in favor of the Declaration, without indicating any personal disagreement.

Question #5 - Wrong Answer Explanations:

A.) The Declaration has been successful in entirely eliminating human rights violations.

Explanation: The passage mentions that the Declaration's effectiveness is questioned, suggesting that it has not been entirely successful in eliminating human rights violations.

C.) The Declaration is entirely ineffective and should be abandoned.

Explanation: The passage does not suggest that the author believes the Declaration is entirely ineffective and should be abandoned.

D.) The Declaration reflects only the values of one culture or society.

Explanation: The passage mentions that critics argue that the Declaration primarily reflects Western values, but does not suggest that the author agrees with this.

Question #6

Correct Answer and Explanations

C.) It outlines the inherent and inviolable rights of all individuals.

Explanation: The passage states in the first paragraph that the Declaration of Human Rights outlines the inherent and inviolable rights of all individuals.

Question #6 - Wrong Answer Explanations:

A.) It was created as a response to the atrocities of World War I.

Explanation: The passage indicates that the Declaration was a response to the atrocities of World War II, not World War I.

B.) It was adopted in the late 19th century.

Explanation: The passage indicates that the Declaration was adopted in 1948, which is not in the late 19th century.

D.) It is primarily supported by Western countries.

Explanation: The passage does not provide information to suggest that the Declaration is primarily supported by Western countries.

Question #7

Correct Answer and Explanations

A.) The declaration has a strong impact on human rights globally.

Explanation: In the context of the passage, "profoundly influential" suggests that the Declaration of Human Rights has had a substantial impact on how human rights are perceived and upheld around the world.

Question #7 - Wrong Answer Explanations:

B.) The declaration has a controversial status.

Explanation: The term "profoundly influential" does not indicate controversy.

C.) The declaration has been revised significantly over time.

Explanation: There is no mention in the passage about significant revisions to the Declaration.

D.) The declaration has been supported by all nations unanimously.

Explanation: The passage does not claim that the declaration has been supported unanimously by all nations.

Question #8

Correct Answer and Explanations

B.) Neutral.

Explanation: The author presents both positive aspects and criticisms of the Declaration of Human Rights, suggesting a neutral attitude rather than one that is overly critical, adulatory, or confused.

Question #8 - Wrong Answer Explanations:

A.) Adulatory.

Explanation: The author does not only praise the declaration, as there are also criticisms presented.

C.) Critical.

Explanation: The author presents criticisms but also discusses positive aspects, indicating a balanced view rather than a solely critical one.

D.) Confused.

Explanation: The author presents an organized discussion of the Declaration, which does not suggest confusion.

Question #9

Correct Answer and Explanations

C.) It does not recognize the inherent rights of all individuals.

Explanation: This criticism is not mentioned in the passage. In fact, the passage states that the Declaration outlines the inherent and inviolable rights of all individuals.

Question #9 - Wrong Answer Explanations:

A.) It primarily reflects Western values.

Explanation: The passage mentions that some critics argue that the Declaration primarily reflects Western values

B.) It has failed to prevent human rights violations.

Explanation: The passage mentions that critics question the effectiveness of the Declaration due to ongoing human rights violations.

D.) Its principles are too universal to be effective.

Explanation: The passage implies that some critics believe that the principles of the Declaration are too universal to be effective.

***

Reading Passage #3

Question #1

Correct Answer and Explanations

B.) They connect individuals with their friends, family, and like-minded people.

Explanation: The passage explicitly mentions this as a primary purpose of social media platforms.

Question #1 - Wrong Answer Explanations:

A.) They promote business development.

Explanation: The passage does not mention business development as a primary benefit of social media.

C.) They provide a platform for advertising and marketing.

Explanation: The passage does not discuss advertising and marketing as a primary benefit of these platforms.

D.) They are the most reliable source of information.

Explanation: The passage highlights the complexities of information dissemination on social media, so it would not categorize them as the most reliable source of information.

Question #2

Correct Answer and Explanations

C.) It is a complex phenomenon with both positive and negative aspects.

Explanation: The author discusses both the positive and negative aspects of social media's role in news dissemination. The passage ends by referring to social media's role as a "complex and paradoxical situation."

Question #2 - Wrong Answer Explanations:

A.) It is a positive development as it reduces dependence on traditional news outlets.

Explanation: This is part of the argument but does not fully encapsulate the author's view.

B.) It is negative as it leads to the spread of misinformation.

Explanation: Similarly, this is part of the argument but does not fully capture the author's view.

D.) It should be restricted to personal use and not be used for sharing news.

Explanation: The author does not suggest that social media should be restricted to personal use.

Question #3

Correct Answer and Explanations

B.) Social media platforms provide equal opportunity for everyone to access and share information.

Explanation: In the context of the passage, "democratized access to information" refers to the idea that social media platforms have allowed more people to access and share information, breaking down barriers that may have existed with traditional news outlets.

Question #3 - Wrong Answer Explanations:

A.) People have the freedom to access any kind of information they want.

Explanation: While this could be inferred as part of the meaning, it does not fully explain the term as used in the passage.

C.) Traditional news outlets no longer have a monopoly on information.

Explanation: This is a possible implication of democratizing access to information, but it does not provide the full context.

D.) Social media platforms are governed by democratic principles.

Explanation: The passage does not suggest that social media platforms are governed by democratic principles.

Question #4

Correct Answer and Explanations

B.) A study found that false information on social media was shared ten times more often than true information.

Explanation: This choice directly strengthens the critics' argument by providing concrete evidence that false information is more widely shared than true information on social media platforms.

Question #4 - Wrong Answer Explanations:

A.) Social media platforms have stricter content moderation policies than traditional news outlets.

Explanation: This does not necessarily strengthen the critics' argument because stricter moderation does not guarantee that false information is not widely spread.

C.) Social media platforms are more accessible than traditional news outlets.

Explanation: The accessibility of social media platforms is not directly related to the critics' argument about the spread of false information.

D.) A significant portion of the global population uses social media.

Explanation: The widespread use of social media does not necessarily strengthen the critics' argument that these platforms can lead to the spread of misinformation.

Question #5

Correct Answer and Explanations

C.) Social media platforms have democratized information by reducing reliance on traditional news outlets.

Explanation: The passage clearly states this point as a common argument made by proponents of social media.

Question #5 - Wrong Answer Explanations:

A.) Social media platforms should be used strictly for entertainment.

Explanation: The passage does not mention that proponents argue for the use of social media strictly for entertainment.

B.) Social media platforms help in better connection with friends and family.

Explanation: While the passage mentions that one of the benefits of social media is connecting with friends and family, it does not state that this is a common argument made by proponents of social media.

D.) Social media platforms should be used strictly for personal communication and not for sharing news.

Explanation: The passage does not mention that proponents argue for the use of social media strictly for personal communication and not for sharing news.

Question #6

Correct Answer and Explanations

C.) Decrease in direct, face-to-face communication.

Explanation: The passage mentions several negative impacts of social media, but it does not mention a decrease in direct, face-to-face communication.

Question #6 - Wrong Answer Explanations:

A.) Increase in the spread of false information.

Explanation: The passage mentions the spread of false information as a potential negative consequence of social media.

B.) Overdependence on social media for news.

Explanation: The passage discusses the overreliance on social media for news as a potential downside.

D.) The creation of ideological echo chambers.

Explanation: The creation of ideological echo chambers is mentioned as a potential negative impact of social media.

Question #7

Correct Answer and Explanations

A.) Traditional news outlets have more rigorous fact-checking processes than social media platforms.

Explanation: The proponents of social media argue that it has democratized information by reducing reliance on traditional news outlets. If traditional news outlets have more rigorous fact-checking processes, this could weaken the proponents' argument by suggesting that the shift away from traditional news outlets may lead to the dissemination of less reliable information.

Question #7 - Wrong Answer Explanations:

B.) Many people still prefer to get their news from traditional outlets.

Explanation: Even if many people still prefer traditional outlets, it doesn't necessarily weaken the argument made by proponents of social media.

C.) False information can still spread on social media even with strict moderation policies.

Explanation: The spread of false information on social media is already acknowledged in the passage, so this point wouldn't weaken the argument made by proponents.

D.) Social media platforms are often used for non-news related activities.

Explanation: The fact that social media platforms are often used for non-news related activities does not directly contradict the argument made by proponents of social media.

***

Reading Passage #4

Question #1

Correct Answer and Explanations

A.) It occurred around 20,000 to 40,000 years ago.

Explanation: The passage provides that "there is considerable evidence to suggest that the domestication of dogs started around 20,000 to 40,000 years ago."

Question #1 - Wrong Answer Explanations:

B.) It is a result of dogs being natural scavengers.

Explanation: The passage states that some view dogs as self-domesticated scavengers, but this is presented as a theory, not a fact.

C.) Humans played a minor role in the process.

Explanation: The passage presents two theories, one of which proposes a significant human role in the domestication of dogs.

D.) It led to the disappearance of wolves.

Explanation: The passage does not suggest that the domestication of dogs led to the disappearance of wolves.

Question #2

Correct Answer and Explanations

A.) Domesticated dogs have smaller teeth and jaws compared to their wolf ancestors.

Explanation: The passage states that "it is often during this era that the physical changes associated with domestication, such as smaller teeth and jaws, become noticeable in canine fossils."

Question #2 - Wrong Answer Explanations:

B.) Dogs have evolved to have a pack mentality and territoriality.

Explanation: The passage suggests that pack mentality and territoriality are behaviors retained from dogs' wolf ancestors, not physical changes due to domestication.

C.) The physical changes were the result of dogs feeding on human waste.

Explanation: The passage does not link the physical changes in dogs to them feeding on human waste.

D.) The physical changes have led to the extinction of some species of the Canidae family.

Explanation: The passage does not connect the physical changes in dogs to the extinction of some Canidae species.

Question #3

Correct Answer and Explanations

B.) They have retained some behavioral traits from their wolf ancestors.

Explanation: The last paragraph of the passage states, "Despite the long history of their domestication, dogs have retained several behavioral traits from their wolf ancestors, such as pack mentality and territoriality."

Question #3 - Wrong Answer Explanations:

A.) They have completely lost all behavioral traits of their wolf ancestors.

Explanation: This contradicts the information in the passage which states that dogs have retained several behaviors from their wolf ancestors.

C.) They have developed a pack mentality due to living with humans.

Explanation: The passage does not suggest that dogs developed a pack mentality due to living with humans. It suggests this trait was retained from their wolf ancestors.

D.) Their behavioral traits have nothing in common with their wolf ancestors.

Explanation: This is contradicted by the passage, which specifically states that dogs have retained some behaviors from their wolf ancestors.

Question #4

Correct Answer and Explanations

C.) To detail the time frame and physical changes associated with dog domestication.

Explanation: The fourth paragraph provides details about when domestication likely started and what physical changes are noticeable in canine fossils from this era, indicating that the purpose is to provide specifics about the domestication process.

Question #4- Wrong Answer Explanations:

A.) To provide evidence supporting the theory that dogs self-domesticated.

Explanation: The fourth paragraph does not specifically support the self-domestication theory.

B.) To criticize the theory that humans played a significant role in dog domestication.

Explanation: The fourth paragraph does not critique any theory of dog domestication.

D.) To argue that domesticated dogs and wolves are completely different species.

Explanation: The passage does not argue that domesticated dogs and wolves are completely different species; instead, it acknowledges their shared ancestry.

Question #5

Correct Answer and Explanations

A.) Dogs adapted to live among humans without direct human intervention.

Explanation: The passage explains self-domestication as a process "whereby wild animals adapt to human environments in the absence of purposeful breeding conducted by humans."

Question #5- Wrong Answer Explanations:

B.) Humans actively bred dogs to promote desirable traits.

Explanation: This answer reflects the opposing theory that the passage discusses - that humans actively intervened in dog domestication. This is not 'self-domestication'.

C.) Wolves voluntarily joined human communities and became dogs.

Explanation: While it's true that wolves might have voluntarily joined human communities, they didn't 'become dogs' instantly. The self-domestication process involved gradual adaptations to the human environment.

D.) Dogs chose to domesticate other animals in their vicinity.

Explanation: The passage does not provide any information to suggest that dogs chose to domesticate other animals in their vicinity.

Question #6

Correct Answer and Explanations

C.) Suggest a point of disagreement or debate regarding dog domestication.

Explanation: The phrase "a bone of contention" is a common idiom used to denote a subject that causes disagreement or argument. In the context of the passage, it refers to the disagreement over theories of dog domestication.

Question #6- Wrong Answer Explanations:

A.) Indicate the skeletal evidence that supports dog domestication theories.

Explanation: The term 'bone of contention' is used figuratively in this context and does not refer to literal bone evidence supporting domestication theories.

B.) Refer to the physical changes dogs underwent during domestication.

Explanation: The phrase 'bone of contention' does not refer to the physical changes dogs underwent during domestication.

D.) Highlight the importance of bones in the diet of ancient dogs.

Explanation: The idiom does not have any connection to the diet of ancient dogs in this context.

***

V
Writing Sample

26

Purpose and Evaluation Criteria

The Writing Sample is a section of the LSAT that assesses your ability to present a coherent and persuasive argument within a limited time frame. This section aims to evaluate your writing skills, analytical reasoning, and ability to organize and develop an argument effectively. Understanding the purpose and evaluation criteria for the Writing Sample is crucial for achieving a strong score in this section.

Purpose of the Writing Sample:

The Writing Sample serves as an opportunity for you to demonstrate your ability to construct a well-structured, reasoned, and persuasive argument. It assesses your capacity to analyze complex issues, evaluate different perspectives, and communicate your thoughts in a clear and concise manner. The Writing Sample is designed to reflect the type of writing you may encounter in law school and legal practice.

Evaluation Criteria:

When evaluating your Writing Sample, the readers consider several key criteria. These include:

Organization and Structure:

- How well you organize your thoughts and present a clear and logical argument.
- The coherence and flow of your ideas, including the use of transitions to guide the reader.

Analysis and Reasoning:

- The quality of your analysis in examining the given decision prompt and the provided options.
- The strength of your reasoning and the logical connection between your premises and conclusion.

Persuasiveness and Support:

- The effectiveness of your persuasive techniques, such as providing relevant examples, evidence, or reasoning to support your argument.
- The ability to anticipate and address potential counterarguments or alternative perspectives.

Clarity and Communication:

- The clarity and precision of your writing, including grammar, vocabulary, and sentence structure.
- The ability to communicate your ideas effectively and concisely.

It is important to note that the Writing Sample is not scored as part of the LSAT's multiple-choice sections. Instead, it is provided to law schools as part of your application, allowing admissions committees to assess your writing abilities.

To excel in the Writing Sample, it is advisable to practice constructing coherent arguments within the time constraints of the exam. Familiarize yourself with the general structure of a persuasive essay and develop a systematic approach for organizing your thoughts and supporting your claims. Practicing with sample prompts and seeking feedback on your writing can also be beneficial in refining your skills.

In this LSAT Prep Guide, we provide guidance on developing strong writing skills, analyzing decision prompts effectively, and constructing persuasive arguments. By understanding the purpose and evaluation criteria for the Writing Sample and practicing your writing abilities, you will be well-prepared to tackle this section with confidence and showcase your writing proficiency to law school admissions committees.

27

Structuring and Organizing a Persuasive Argument

In the Writing Sample section of the LSAT, the ability to structure and organize a persuasive argument effectively is essential for achieving a strong score. This section provides tips and strategies to help you structure and organize your persuasive argument in a clear and compelling manner.

Understand the Prompt:

- Carefully read and analyze the given decision prompt to fully grasp its requirements and the choices presented.
- Identify the main issue or question at hand, as well as any key factors or considerations that need to be addressed.

Outline Your Argument:

- Develop a clear and concise thesis statement that states your position or preferred option.
- Outline the main points or arguments that support your thesis statement.
- Consider the logical flow of your arguments and the order in which you present them.

Introduction:

- Begin with an engaging introduction that provides context and sets the stage for your argument.
- Clearly state your thesis statement to establish the position or option you are advocating for.

Body Paragraphs:

- Dedicate each body paragraph to a specific supporting argument or point.
- Present your arguments in a logical order, arranging them from strongest to weakest or in a manner that best builds your case.
- Provide evidence, examples, or reasoning to support each argument and strengthen its validity.
- Use topic sentences and transitions to create cohesion and guide the reader through your argument.

Address Counterarguments:

- Anticipate and address potential counterarguments or alternative perspectives.
- Refute opposing viewpoints by presenting compelling counterarguments supported by evidence or reasoning.
- Acknowledge potential limitations or weaknesses in your argument and provide rebuttals or clarifications.

Conclusion:

- Summarize your main arguments and restate your thesis statement in a concise manner.
- Leave a lasting impression by providing a compelling closing statement that reinforces the strength of your position.

Clarity and Coherence:

- Use clear and precise language to convey your ideas effectively.
- Ensure that your argument flows logically and coherently from one point to another.
- Avoid excessive jargon or complex language that may hinder comprehension.

Proofread and Revise:

- Allocate time to proofread your essay for grammar, punctuation, and spelling errors.
- Review the clarity and coherence of your argument, making any necessary revisions to improve its overall effectiveness.

By implementing these tips, you can structure and organize your persuasive argument in a manner that engages the reader and effectively communicates your position. Regular practice with sample prompts and seeking feedback on your writing can further refine your skills and enhance your ability to construct persuasive arguments within the time constraints of the LSAT.

In this LSAT Prep Guide, we provide guidance on structuring persuasive arguments, analyzing decision prompts, and developing strong writing skills. By applying these strategies and practicing your writing abilities, you will be well-equipped to tackle the Writing Sample section with confidence and demonstrate your persuasive writing proficiency to law school admissions committees.

28

Techniques for Developing Coherent Analysis within Time Constraints

In the Writing Sample section of the LSAT, the ability to develop a coherent analysis within the given time constraints is crucial for presenting a well-constructed and persuasive argument. This section provides techniques to help you effectively develop a coherent analysis while managing your time efficiently.

Understand the Prompt Quickly:

- Read the decision prompt carefully and identify the main issue or question it presents.
- Skim the provided options to gain a general understanding of the choices available.
- Quickly assess the context and scope of the prompt to determine your approach.

Plan Your Response:

- Take a moment to outline the structure of your response.
- Determine the key points or arguments you want to address and the order in which you will present them.
- Consider the time you have available and allocate it accordingly to ensure a balanced and well-developed analysis.

Focus on Key Elements:

- Identify the critical elements of the prompt that require analysis, such as relevant factors, assumptions, or implications.
- Prioritize your analysis by focusing on the most significant aspects that support your argument.

Analyze Methodically:

- Present a clear and concise introduction that establishes the context and provides an overview of your analysis.
- Break down the prompt into manageable components and address them systematically.
- Analyze each component thoroughly, considering its implications, consequences, and logical connections to other elements.
- Support your analysis with relevant examples, evidence, or reasoning to strengthen your arguments.

Stay on Track:

- Remain focused on the main question or issue presented in the prompt.
- Avoid getting sidetracked by tangential or irrelevant information.
- Continually refer back to your outline and ensure that your analysis aligns with your initial plan.

Manage Your Time Effectively:

- Keep track of the time allotted for the Writing Sample and pace yourself accordingly.
- Allocate sufficient time for each section of your analysis, ensuring that you have ample opportunity to present and support your arguments.
- Be mindful of time-consuming tangents and make adjustments to maintain a balance between depth and coverage of your analysis.

Revise and Edit Strategically:

- As time allows, review your analysis for clarity, coherence, and logical progression.
- Make necessary revisions to refine your arguments, improve sentence structure, and eliminate any errors.
- Prioritize revisions based on their impact on the overall effectiveness of your analysis.

By implementing these techniques, you can develop a coherent analysis within the time constraints of the Writing Sample section. Regular practice with timed writing exercises, focusing on concise and efficient analysis, will help you refine your skills and improve your ability to present a well-constructed argument under pressure.

In this LSAT Prep Guide, we provide guidance on developing coherent analyses, analyzing decision prompts effectively, and managing time constraints. By practicing these techniques and honing your writing abilities, you will be well-prepared to tackle the Writing Sample section with confidence, delivering a strong and well-structured analysis within the allotted time frame.

29

Writing Sample Criteria

There is typically one Writing Sample question included as part of the exam. This section presents a decision prompt and requires test takers to construct a persuasive argument within a 35-minute time limit. The Writing Sample is unscored and serves as an opportunity for law schools to assess your writing and analytical abilities. It is important to note that while the Writing Sample is an integral part of the LSAT, it does not contribute to your overall LSAT score.

30

Practice Exercise 1

There is typically one Writing Sample question included as part of the exam. This section presents a decision prompt and requires test takers to construct a persuasive argument within a 35-minute time limit. The Writing Sample is unscored and serves as an opportunity for law schools to assess your writing and analytical abilities. It is important to note that while the Writing Sample is an integral part of the LSAT, it does not contribute to your overall LSAT score.

Writing Sample Exercise #1

Greenwood City is looking for ways to improve its downtown area. After much deliberation, the city council has narrowed down their options to two redevelopment plans.

Plan A suggests converting an old, vacant factory into a community arts center. This center would provide space for art exhibitions, art classes, and other cultural events. Advocates argue that it would provide a platform for local artists and attract tourists, which would boost the city's economy.

Plan B proposes transforming the factory into a shopping complex with retail stores, restaurants, and a multi-level parking garage. Supporters believe this option would create jobs and stimulate economic growth more directly.

Your task is to choose one of the plans and defend your choice. Please make sure to address both the advantages and disadvantages of your chosen plan and why you believe it is more beneficial than the other option.

31

Practice Exercise 2

There is typically one Writing Sample question included as part of the exam. This section presents a decision prompt and requires test takers to construct a persuasive argument within a 35-minute time limit. The Writing Sample is unscored and serves as an opportunity for law schools to assess your writing and analytical abilities. It is important to note that while the Writing Sample is an integral part of the LSAT, it does not contribute to your overall LSAT score.

<u>Writing Sample Exercise #2</u>

The board of directors of a growing startup company is considering two options for its next round of expansion. The company, TechGen, specializes in developing software solutions for various industries, including healthcare, finance, and education.

Option 1: To expand their physical operations by opening offices in four new cities. Proponents argue that having a physical presence in these cities would make the company more accessible to clients in these regions, improving relationships and boosting sales. This would also provide more job opportunities to the locals in those areas. However, critics point out that this would require significant upfront capital, and the ongoing costs of maintaining physical offices can be high.

Option 2: To invest in virtual reality (VR) technology and create virtual offices that allow employees to collaborate from anywhere in the world. Advocates say that this would save on the high costs of physical expansion and create a unique, innovative working environment that could attract top talent. However, opponents argue that VR technology is still developing, and significant investment would be required. Moreover, potential clients may prefer traditional in-person interactions.

In making a decision, the board of directors has to consider the long-term growth of the company, its financial viability, the company's image, and the impact on both clients and employees.

Write an essay in which you argue for one option over the other based on the given criteria. Be sure to address both the potential benefits and drawbacks of your chosen option.

32

Practice Exercise 1: Sample Writing Answers

<u>Writing Sample Exercise #1 - Option A</u>

Plan A suggests converting an old, vacant factory into a community arts center. This center would provide space for art exhibitions, art classes, and other cultural events. Advocates argue that it would provide a platform for local artists and attract tourists, which would boost the city's economy.

<u>Sample Answer:</u>

Greenwood City should adopt Plan A, which suggests converting the vacant factory into a community arts center. There are several compelling reasons for this choice, even when acknowledging the potential benefits of Plan B.

Firstly, the establishment of a community arts center would serve to promote the local arts scene. Artists, both established and budding, would be provided with a platform to showcase their work. The center could hold regular exhibitions, enabling these artists to gain exposure and recognition. Furthermore, this art center would foster a vibrant cultural environment by offering art classes and hosting cultural events. It would also enrich the lives of the city's residents, providing them with opportunities for creative expression and cultural participation.

Secondly, the arts center would act as an attraction for tourists. Many cities around the world have experienced a significant increase in tourism owing to their art and culture scenes. Tourists drawn to the arts center would not only boost revenue through ticket sales but also stimulate the broader local economy. They would patronize local businesses such as hotels, restaurants, and shops, which could spur more economic growth than a shopping complex alone.

In contrast, Plan B's proposal to transform the factory into a retail complex could certainly create jobs and stimulate economic growth. However, the long-term viability of such a plan is uncertain. With the rise of online shopping and the decline of brick-and-mortar retail, betting the city's future on a retail complex could be a risky move.

It is also worth noting that while both plans would generate economic benefits, the arts center has the added advantage of contributing to the city's social capital. By fostering a strong sense of community and civic pride, the arts center could pay dividends that extend far beyond the immediate economic impact.

Lastly, the transformation of the vacant factory into an arts center could serve as a symbol of the city's commitment to preserving its history and identity, something a generic shopping complex might fail to achieve. The architecture and industrial aesthetic of the old factory, combined with the new purpose of promoting art, could create a unique space that captures the city's past and its future.

In conclusion, while both plans have potential benefits, Plan A would likely offer a broader range of economic, social, and cultural returns on investment. It represents a holistic approach to urban development, one that values not only economic growth but also the enrichment of local culture and community.

* * *

Writing Sample Exercise #1 - Option B

Plan B proposes transforming the factory into a shopping complex with retail stores, restaurants, and a multi-level parking garage. Supporters believe this option would create jobs and stimulate economic growth more directly.

Sample Answer:

Plan B, which advocates for the conversion of the vacant factory into a retail complex, presents Greenwood City with a robust strategy for economic development. While the alternative Plan A to create a community arts center also has merits, a variety of reasons lend more weight to the decision for the retail complex.

Primarily, a retail complex would likely create a significant number of jobs. These would range from positions within individual retail outlets to roles in security, maintenance, and administration. Furthermore, the increased commerce could stimulate the creation of additional jobs in the broader community, particularly in areas such as transportation, catering, and other services linked to retail.

Secondly, the steady revenue generated from rents, sales taxes, and other fees associated with a retail complex would be beneficial for Greenwood City's financial health. This income could be reinvested in the community, perhaps funding public services such as education, healthcare, and infrastructure. Over time, this reinvestment could lead to a higher standard of living and a more prosperous city.

While Plan A's arts center may attract tourists interested in culture, the retail complex's appeal could be broader, attracting both local shoppers and tourists. In the face of increased online shopping, many retail complexes have successfully reinvented themselves as destinations offering unique shopping experiences and a variety of entertainment and dining options, thus ensuring their continued viability.

Furthermore, the retail complex could become an integral part of the community by hosting local events and gatherings, thus contributing to the community's social fabric, much like the proposed arts center. Many retail complexes host seasonal events, farmers' markets, and charity fundraisers, becoming a hub for community activities.

It is also worth noting that a thriving retail complex does not preclude the promotion of local culture. Retail outlets could sell locally produced goods and artwork, thereby supporting local artisans. Spaces within the complex could be used for art exhibits, concerts, or cultural performances, providing some of the same benefits as the proposed arts center, but within a more commercially viable framework.

In conclusion, while both plans present potential advantages, Plan B's retail complex provides a more immediate, tangible, and sustainable economic impact. It promises job creation, steady revenue for the city, a broader appeal to locals and tourists, and the potential to support local culture - all while offering the community a social gathering place. Therefore, adopting Plan B would likely yield the most benefits for Greenwood City.

* * *

33

Practice Exercise 2: Sample Writing Answers

<u>Writing Sample Exercise #2 - Option #1</u>

The Imperative of Physical Expansion for Sustainable Growth

The decision facing TechGen's board of directors—whether to expand physical operations by opening offices in four new cities, or to invest in Virtual Reality (VR) technology for creating virtual offices—has far-reaching implications for the company's future. While both options have their merits and challenges, Option 1, expanding physical operations, is a more strategic choice for TechGen, when considering long-term growth, financial viability, the company's image, and the impact on both clients and employees.

<u>Sample Answer:</u>

Option 1: To expand their physical operations by opening offices in four new cities. Proponents argue that having a physical presence in these cities would make the company more accessible to clients in these regions, improving relationships and boosting sales. This would also provide more job opportunities to the locals in those areas. However, critics point out that this would require significant upfront capital, and the ongoing costs of maintaining physical offices can be high.

Firstly, in terms of long-term growth, having a physical presence in four new cities provides tangible growth and a real footprint in the industry. It allows TechGen to more directly penetrate local markets, enhance client relationships and boost sales. TechGen can interact more closely with its clients, providing personalized service that builds trust and loyalty. Moreover, expansion into new geographical locations opens up the prospect for capturing market share from regional competitors, thus solidifying TechGen's industry standing.

Financial viability is, of course, a crucial concern. It's undeniable that setting up physical offices entails significant upfront capital and ongoing maintenance costs. However, these costs must be seen as an investment that will yield substantial returns over time. The increased sales from improved client relationships, as well as the potential for attracting new clients in these regions, should outweigh the costs in the long run.

The company's image is another vital factor to consider. A physical presence enhances a company's prestige and demonstrates a level of commitment and permanence that a virtual office simply can't match. Clients, stakeholders, and even employees tend to trust businesses with a physical presence more, as it provides a sense of stability and credibility.

The impact on employees should not be overlooked. Opening new offices would not only provide more job opportunities to locals but would also give current employees room for growth, such as opportunities for relocation or promotion. While VR could offer some innovative working conditions, it may also create a sense of isolation amongst employees who lack face-to-face interaction.

The proposed alternative, investing in VR technology, indeed has its allure. However, the technology is still in its infancy, and its acceptance as a standard workplace environment is far from mainstream. Investing heavily in an unproven area carries considerable risk, and relying on it could alienate clients who prefer traditional modes of interaction.

In conclusion, while both options have potential, Option 1's promise of tangible growth, enhanced client relationships, improved company image, and positive impact on employees make it the most viable choice for TechGen. It's an investment in the company's future that will pay dividends in sustainable, long-term growth and market dominance.

***

Writing Sample Exercise #2 - Option #2

Option 2: To invest in virtual reality (VR) technology and create virtual offices that allow employees to collaborate from anywhere in the world. Advocates say that this would save on the high costs of physical expansion and create a unique, innovative working environment that could attract top talent. However, opponents argue that VR technology is still developing, and significant investment would be required. Moreover, potential clients may prefer traditional in-person interactions.

Sample Answer:

Embracing the Digital Future: The Case for Virtual Offices

In the choice between expanding physical operations or investing in Virtual Reality (VR) technology to establish virtual offices, TechGen faces a pivotal decision that will shape its future. Both options come with opportunities and challenges, yet, option 2—embracing VR technology—provides a more innovative, cost-effective, and sustainable path forward, considering the evolving landscape of the tech industry, financial considerations, the ability to attract top talent, and the potential to enhance productivity.

From an industry perspective, adopting VR technology would position TechGen as a pioneer, embracing the digital future of workplaces. This move would undoubtedly align with TechGen's image as a tech-forward company, enhancing its reputation and enabling it to stand out from competitors. By leading the charge in this burgeoning field, TechGen would not just be following trends but setting them, signaling to clients and competitors alike that it is at the cutting edge of technological innovation.

On a financial front, VR technology presents a significantly more cost-effective solution compared to the heavy upfront and ongoing costs of physical offices. Establishing virtual offices eliminates the need for real estate investments, office maintenance costs, and commuting expenses for employees. Furthermore, VR technology is scalable, allowing for expansion without the proportional increase in costs associated with physical locations.

One of the most compelling reasons to invest in VR is the opportunity to attract and retain a broader pool of talent. Virtual offices are not confined by geographical boundaries, enabling TechGen to hire the best talent from around the globe. This diverse and talented workforce will not only contribute to TechGen's productivity but also foster innovation and creativity. Moreover, the flexibility of virtual workplaces has been proven to enhance employee satisfaction, leading to higher retention rates.

The use of VR technology could also enhance productivity and efficiency. Advanced VR platforms allow for seamless collaboration, interactive meetings, and immersive presentations that could be more engaging than traditional formats. The elimination of commuting time could also result in more effective work hours.

The alternative of physical expansion, while familiar, is less advantageous. In addition to the heavy costs, it is a relatively standard approach that does not set TechGen apart from its competitors. It also limits the talent pool to specific locations and may not appeal to the increasing number of employees seeking flexible work arrangements.

In conclusion, while both options present potential paths for TechGen, option 2's promise of innovation, cost-effectiveness, global talent acquisition, and productivity enhancement presents a more compelling case. It represents a strategic investment that not only aligns with the tech industry's future but also positions TechGen as a trailblazer in this new digital frontier.

***

VI
LSAT Test Best Practices

34

Test Day Tips for Optimal Performance and Stress Management

Taking the LSAT is a significant undertaking that requires both mental preparedness and effective stress management on test day. This section provides test day tips to help you achieve optimal performance and navigate the exam with confidence.

Get Adequate Rest:

- Ensure you get a good night's sleep before the test day to feel refreshed and alert.

Avoid studying intensely on the day before the exam; focus on relaxation and mental preparation instead.

Arrive Early and Be Prepared:

- Plan your travel to the test center in advance, allowing extra time for unexpected delays.
- Bring all necessary test materials, including your LSAT admission ticket, valid photo ID, pencils, and erasers.
- Familiarize yourself with the test center's location, facilities, and parking options beforehand.

Follow Test Instructions:

- Carefully listen to and read all instructions provided by the test administrators.
- Understand the timing for each section and be aware of the start and end times for breaks.

Pace Yourself:

- The LSAT is a timed exam, so it's essential to manage your time wisely.
- If you encounter a challenging question, consider skipping it temporarily and revisiting it later if time permits.
- Avoid spending too much time on any single question, as it may prevent you from completing other sections.

Stay Focused and Calm:

- Maintain a positive mindset throughout the exam.
- If you encounter a difficult question, remain calm and move on to the next one.
  - Dwelling on a challenging question can affect your overall performance.

Utilize Breaks Wisely:

- Take advantage of the provided breaks between sections to rest, clear your mind, and stretch.
- Avoid discussing the test with other test-takers during the break, as it might increase stress or create unnecessary distractions.

Use Scratch Paper Effectively:

- Use the scratch paper provided to jot down notes, diagrams, or outlines for logical reasoning and logic games sections.
- Organizing your thoughts on scratch paper can help you approach questions more effectively.

Avoid Guessing Blindly:

- While educated guessing can be beneficial, avoid guessing blindly when you are unsure of an answer.
- Guessing without any reasoning might lead to unnecessary deductions due to incorrect answers.

Stay Hydrated and Nourished:

- Bring water and a light snack to stay hydrated and energized during the exam.
  - Avoid heavy or sugary foods that might cause energy fluctuations.

Stay until the End:

- Utilize all the allotted time for each section, as unanswered questions receive no credit.
- Even if you find yourself running out of time, make sure to fill in an answer for every question.

By implementing these test day tips, you can enhance your performance and reduce stress during the LSAT. Maintaining composure and utilizing effective strategies will contribute to a more successful and confident test-taking experience.

In this LSAT Prep Guide, we provide guidance on test-taking strategies, time management, and stress reduction techniques to help you achieve your best performance on the LSAT. By combining these tips with thorough preparation, you will be well-prepared to tackle the exam and showcase your abilities to their fullest potential.

35

Time Management Techniques for Each Section

Effective time management is critical for success on the LSAT. This section provides time management techniques tailored to each section of the exam, helping you maximize your performance and complete each section within the allotted time.

Logical Reasoning:

- Pace Yourself: Logical Reasoning consists of two sections, each with approximately 25 questions to be completed within 35 minutes. Aim to spend about 1 minute and 20 seconds on each question.
- Prioritize Question Types: If you find certain question types more challenging, consider flagging them and returning to them later. Focus on answering questions you are more confident about first.
- Skip Strategically: If you encounter a particularly difficult question, avoid getting stuck. Mark it, and move on to the next one. Revisit marked questions in the remaining time.

Analytical Reasoning (Logic Games):

- Divide Your Time: The Logic Games section consists of approximately 23 questions to be completed within 35 minutes. Allocate roughly 1 minute and 30 seconds per question.
- Create Efficient Diagrams: Use clear and efficient diagramming techniques to represent the game's rules and elements accurately. This will help you quickly solve the questions.
- Triage the Games: Skim through the four games at the beginning and identify the one you find easiest. Start with that game, then move on to the others based on difficulty.

Reading Comprehension:

- Time Allocation: The Reading Comprehension section typically includes four passages, with 5-8 questions per passage. Allocate approximately 8 minutes per passage.

- Active Reading: Engage actively with the passage, underlining key points, main ideas, and supporting evidence. This will aid in quicker comprehension and answering questions efficiently.
- Prioritize Passages: If you find a particular passage challenging, consider starting with the easier ones and returning to the more difficult passage later.

Writing Sample:

- Time Management: The Writing Sample requires you to write a persuasive essay in 35 minutes. Allocate a few minutes at the beginning to plan your response and outline your argument.
- Structure Your Essay: Begin with a clear introduction, followed by well-organized body paragraphs supporting your thesis, and conclude with a concise summary.
- Stay Focused: While the Writing Sample is unscored, using your time wisely will help you present a well-structured and persuasive argument.

Overall Time Management Tips:

- Practice Timing: During your LSAT preparation, practice answering questions and sections under timed conditions to build your pacing skills.
- Use Practice Tests: Take full-length LSAT practice tests to simulate the test day experience and identify areas where time management can be improved.
- Maintain Focus: Avoid spending too much time on individual questions or becoming preoccupied with perfection. Keep moving through each section steadily.

By implementing these time management techniques, you can confidently approach each section of the LSAT, ensuring that you make the best use of your allotted time and achieve your best performance on the exam.

In this LSAT Prep Guide, we provide further guidance on time management strategies, tailored to each section, to help you optimize your performance on the LSAT. Combining these techniques with consistent practice will empower you to navigate the exam with efficiency and precision.

36
Guessing Strategies and the Impact on Scoring

The LSAT employs a scoring system that rewards correct answers while not penalizing for incorrect answers. As such, strategic guessing can play a significant role in optimizing your LSAT score. This section outlines guessing strategies and the potential impact on your overall scoring.

Educated Guessing:

- When faced with a challenging question, consider making an educated guess based on your knowledge, reasoning, and elimination of clearly incorrect choices.
- Review any clues or context within the question that might help you make an educated guess.

Time Management:

- If you encounter a particularly difficult question, avoid getting stuck and consuming excessive time. Instead, make an educated guess and move on to other questions.
- Manage your time wisely to ensure you have sufficient opportunity to address all questions.

Elimination Techniques:

- Use the process of elimination to rule out obviously incorrect answer choices.
- Narrowing down options increases the probability of guessing correctly if you are unsure of the answer.

No Blank Answers:

- The LSAT does not penalize for incorrect answers, so it is crucial to provide an answer for every question, even if you are unsure.
- Leaving questions blank guarantees zero credit, while guessing offers the possibility of earning points.

Weighting of Scores:

- The LSAT's scoring system takes into account the number of correct answers. Incorrect answers do not contribute to your score, but unanswered questions have no impact on your score.
- By making educated guesses, you increase the likelihood of selecting correct answers and improving your overall score.

Blind Guessing:

- While educated guessing is beneficial, blind guessing (randomly selecting an answer without any reasoning) is not recommended, as it offers no advantage over leaving questions blank.
- If you are unsure of an answer and cannot eliminate any choices, it may be better to skip the question.

Pattern Avoidance:

- Avoid falling into predictable patterns while guessing. The LSAT employs various methods to disrupt patterns in answer choices, making it challenging to guess solely based on pattern recognition.

Remember that the LSAT is a standardized test with a strict time limit. While strategic guessing can enhance your chances of selecting correct answers, it is essential to use guessing techniques judiciously. Making educated guesses and managing your time effectively can help you maximize your score, particularly when facing difficult or time-consuming questions.

In this LSAT Prep Guide, we provide further guidance on guessing strategies and their impact on scoring. By integrating these strategies into your LSAT preparation and practice, you can approach the exam with confidence and optimize your scoring potential.

37
Strategies for Reviewing and Analyzing Practice Tests

Reviewing and analyzing practice tests is a crucial component of LSAT preparation. This section provides strategies to help you make the most of your practice test performance, identify areas for improvement, and refine your test-taking skills.

Review with a Critical Eye:

- After completing a practice test, review it thoroughly with a critical mindset.
- Identify questions you answered correctly and those you answered incorrectly.

Analyze Incorrect Answers:
- Focus on understanding why you selected incorrect answers. Identify any patterns or common errors in your reasoning.
- Examine the questions and answer choices to determine the correct approach and the specific reasoning required for accurate responses.

Identify Weak Areas:

- Pay attention to sections or question types where you consistently struggle.
- Prioritize the improvement of weaker areas in subsequent practice sessions.

Timing Analysis:

- Evaluate your time management during the practice test.
- Identify sections or questions where you spent too much time or felt rushed.
- Practice pacing yourself to ensure completion of all questions within the allotted time.

Keep an Error Log:

- Maintain an error log to record the types of questions you tend to answer incorrectly.
- Note the reasons behind your mistakes and the corrective measures you intend to take in future practice.

- Use the insights from your practice test review to create a targeted study plan.
- Dedicate more time to practicing areas in which you need improvement.

Review Correct Answers:
- Revisit questions you answered correctly to ensure you understand the reasoning behind your choices.
- Confirm that your reasoning aligns with the correct approach to reinforce your understanding.

Simulate Test Conditions:

- Practice under timed conditions to replicate the test day experience.
- Familiarize yourself with the pressure of adhering to time constraints.

Take Multiple Practice Tests:

- Take several practice tests throughout your LSAT preparation journey.
- Consistent practice will improve your familiarity with the exam format and enhance your ability to perform under test conditions.

Track Progress:

- Monitor your progress over time by comparing your scores and performance in subsequent practice tests.
- Celebrate improvements and use setbacks as learning opportunities.

Seek Feedback:

- If possible, seek feedback from experienced LSAT tutors or instructors.
- External insights can provide valuable guidance and help address specific areas of improvement.

By employing these strategies for reviewing and analyzing practice tests, you can pinpoint areas of strength and weakness in your LSAT preparation. Regular and targeted practice, coupled with thoughtful analysis, will enhance your test-taking skills, confidence, and readiness for the actual LSAT.

In this LSAT Prep Guide, we provide further guidance on effective review techniques and strategies for continual improvement. By integrating these strategies into your preparation routine, you can optimize your performance and approach the LSAT with a strong foundation of knowledge and skill.

VI
Conclusion

38

Key Takeaways and Strategies Covered in the Guide

Throughout this comprehensive LSAT Prep Guide, we have provided you with essential insights, strategies, and techniques to help you prepare effectively for the LSAT. As you approach the conclusion of this guide, let's recap the key takeaways and strategies covered:

LSAT Importance: The LSAT plays a crucial role in law school admissions, assessing critical thinking, analytical reasoning, logical reasoning, and reading comprehension skills.

Benefits of Comprehensive Preparation: A comprehensive LSAT preparation guide equips you with effective strategies, enhances critical skills, and fosters confidence in tackling the exam.

Guide Objectives and Structure: The LSAT Essentials guide is structured to align with the LSAT's test sections, covering Logical Reasoning, Analytical Reasoning (Logic Games), Reading Comprehension, and the Writing Sample. Each section focuses on specific objectives to ensure a systematic and well-rounded approach to LSAT preparation.

Logical Reasoning: Strategies for understanding question types, analyzing arguments, and approaching various question types to increase accuracy.

Analytical Reasoning (Logic Games): Techniques for diagramming and solving different types of logic games to maximize efficiency and accuracy.

Reading Comprehension: Active reading strategies and approaches for identifying main ideas, structures, and the author's perspective to improve comprehension and answer accuracy.

Writing Sample: Tips for structuring and organizing a persuasive argument within the time constraints of the Writing Sample section.

LSAT Test Strategies: Test day tips for optimal performance and stress management, time management techniques for each section, guessing strategies, and reviewing and analyzing practice tests effectively.

By diligently applying the strategies and techniques outlined in this guide, you can confidently navigate the LSAT and showcase your full potential to law schools. Remember to practice regularly, utilize official LSAC resources, and seek support through online communities or professional LSAT courses if needed.

Success on the LSAT demands dedication, disciplined preparation, and a proactive approach. Continue to build your knowledge, refine your skills, and maintain a positive mindset throughout your LSAT journey.

As you embark on this important chapter in your academic and professional pursuits, we wish you the utmost success in your LSAT preparation and future endeavors in the legal field. Stay focused, determined, and prepared, and may your efforts lead to an exceptional performance on the LSAT and a promising future in law.

39

Final LSAT Success Advice

As you approach the LSAT, we understand the significance of this pivotal moment in your journey towards pursuing a legal career. The LSAT is a demanding exam, but with diligent preparation and a positive mindset, you have the potential to excel and secure your path to law school.

Here are some final words of encouragement and advice to guide you toward LSAT success:

Believe in Yourself: Trust in your abilities and the hard work you have invested in your LSAT preparation. Self-confidence is essential in tackling challenging questions and staying focused during the exam.

Embrace Challenges: The LSAT is designed to challenge your critical thinking and analytical skills. Embrace the complexity of the questions as an opportunity to showcase your intellectual aptitude.

Stay Committed to Preparation: Consistent and dedicated preparation is the key to LSAT success. Continuously engage with practice tests, review materials, and resources to enhance your skills.

Practice Under Test Conditions: To replicate the actual test experience, practice under timed conditions. Familiarity with the time constraints will boost your confidence on test day.

Prioritize Time Management: Allocate time effectively for each section and question. Time management is crucial to ensuring that you can address all questions thoroughly.

Learn from Mistakes: Embrace mistakes as learning opportunities. Analyze incorrect answers, identify patterns, and work on improving your weaknesses.

Balance Accuracy and Pacing: Strive for accuracy while also managing your pace. Aim to answer as many questions correctly as possible while utilizing educated guessing for challenging questions.

Seek Support: If you encounter difficulties, consider seeking support from LSAT instructors, tutors, or online communities. Learning from others' insights can help you refine your strategies.

Maintain a Positive Mindset: Test day can be stressful, but maintaining a positive mindset will keep you focused and composed. Approach the exam with determination and optimism.

Remember Your Goals: Keep in mind the long-term goals driving your pursuit of law school. Let your aspirations fuel your motivation and commitment to succeed.

As you move forward in your LSAT journey, remember that LSAT scores are just one aspect of your law school application. Admissions committees also consider your academic achievements, personal statement, letters of recommendation, and extracurricular activities. Combined with a strong LSAT score, these elements present a holistic view of your potential as a law school candidate.

Stay disciplined, persevere through challenges, and approach the LSAT with a clear focus on success. Your preparation and dedication will undoubtedly pay off, and you will be well-prepared to excel on the LSAT and take the next steps towards a rewarding legal career.

Best of luck on your LSAT journey, and may your hard work lead you to a future of academic achievement and professional fulfillment in the field of law.

40

Continued Practice and Self-Assessment for Improvement

As you conclude your journey through this LSAT Prep Guide, it is essential to recognize the ongoing commitment to practice and self-assessment as crucial elements for continual improvement in LSAT preparation.

The LSAT is a challenging exam that demands not only mastery of the content but also the refinement of critical thinking and analytical skills. Continued practice is the key to reinforcing your knowledge, honing your strategies, and building confidence in your abilities.

Embrace the significance of continued practice in the following ways:

Reinforcing Concepts: Regular practice solidifies your understanding of the LSAT's question types, formats, and techniques. Repetition enhances your ability to recognize patterns and apply strategies effectively.

Enhancing Speed and Accuracy: Practice under timed conditions aids in developing efficiency and accuracy. Gradually, you will become adept at answering questions within the time constraints of each section.

Identifying Areas for Improvement: Ongoing practice allows you to identify areas where you can further enhance your skills. Consistent self-assessment empowers you to focus on your weaknesses and target them for improvement.

Building Endurance: The LSAT is a lengthy exam, and stamina is essential for maintaining focus throughout the entire test. Regular practice will improve your test-taking endurance.

Gaining Confidence: As you observe your progress through practice tests and review sessions, you will gain confidence in your abilities, bolstering your readiness for the actual exam.

Additionally, self-assessment is a valuable tool for identifying your strengths and areas needing improvement. Incorporate self-assessment into your LSAT preparation in the following ways:

Reviewing Practice Tests: Carefully review each practice test, analyzing both correct and incorrect answers. Identify patterns in your reasoning and learn from your mistakes.

Tracking Progress: Keep a record of your scores, timing, and performance over time. Monitor improvements and identify areas where further growth is required.

Evaluating Strategies: Assess the effectiveness of the strategies and techniques you have applied during your LSAT preparation. Determine what works best for you and adjust accordingly.

Seeking Feedback: If possible, seek feedback from experienced LSAT instructors or study partners. External insights can provide valuable perspectives on areas for improvement.

By embracing the importance of continued practice and self-assessment, you will transform your LSAT preparation into a dynamic and personalized learning journey. Consistent practice and evaluation will drive your progress and readiness to face the LSAT with confidence.

As you embark on this transformative path, remember that your dedication, perseverance, and commitment to improvement are key to achieving your desired LSAT score. The LSAT is a stepping stone to your legal career, and by continuously refining your skills, you will pave the way to a successful future in the legal profession.

We wish you the best in your LSAT preparation and the exciting opportunities that await you beyond this critical examination. May your journey be filled with growth, learning, and eventual triumph on the LSAT and in your pursuit of a fulfilling legal career.

Made in the USA
Las Vegas, NV
18 October 2023